A CONTRIBUTION TO

THE GENERAL EQUILIBRIUM THEORY
OF PREFERENTIAL TRADING

CONTRIBUTIONS
TO
ECONOMIC ANALYSIS

61

Edited by

J. JOHNSTON

J. SANDEE

R. H. STROTZ

J. TINBERGEN

P. J. VERDOORN

NORTH-HOLLAND PUBLISHING COMPANY
AMSTERDAM · LONDON

A CONTRIBUTION TO

THE GENERAL EQUILIBRIUM THEORY OF PREFERENTIAL TRADING

by

MURRAY C. KEMP

University of New South Wales

1969

NORTH-HOLLAND PUBLISHING COMPANY
AMSTERDAM · LONDON

Library of Congress Catalog Card Number: 72–101553
SBN: 7204 3162 X

Publishers:

NORTH-HOLLAND PUBLISHING COMPANY – AMSTERDAM
NORTH-HOLLAND PUBLISHING COMPANY, LTD. – LONDON

PRINTED IN THE NETHERLANDS

Introduction to the series

This series consists of a number of hitherto unpublished studies, which are introduced by the editors in the belief that they represent fresh contributions to economic science.

The term *economic analysis* as used in the title of the series has been adopted because it covers both the activities of the theoretical economist and the research worker.

Although the analytical methods used by the various contributors are not the same, they are nevertheless conditioned by the common origin of their studies, namely theoretical problems encountered in practical research. Since for this reason, business cycle research and national accounting, research work on behalf of economic policy, and problems of planning are the main sources of the subjects dealt with, they necessarily determine the manner of approach adopted by the authors. Their methods tend to be 'practical' in the sense of not being too far remote from application to actual economic conditions. In addition they are quantitative rather than qualitative.

It is the hope of the editors that the publication of these studies will help to stimulate the exchange of scientific information and to reinforce international cooperation in the field of economics.

THE EDITORS

Foreword

Problems associated with international economic integration have in the past twenty years been the subject of intensive debate. The debate has proceeded at several levels: popular and professional, political and technical. The debate has however been discursive and shapeless, lacking an agreed formal framework.

Professor Murray Kemp's book contains a theoretical analysis of several carefully defined problems associated with international economic integration. The point of view adopted throughout is that of general equilibrium. The book will not be the last word; many important issues of a monetary or dynamic character are not treated. It is my hope however that the book will serve as a stimulus to further professional discussion, and that it will influence the shape taken by that discussion.

INGVAR SVENNILSON
Institute for International
Economic Studies
University of Stockholm, July 1969

Preface

In this short book I examine the effects on international trade and investment and on levels of national welfare of the concerted adjustment by a group of countries of the obstacles and incentives to the movement of goods and factors between them.

In reviewing the professional and journalistic literature on preferential trading arrangements I have been struck by the fragmentary and partial-equilibrium character of the formal models employed. Especially notable is the absence of any systematic analysis of the connections between tariff policy and international factor movements. The poverty of the theory is the more puzzling in that almost all of it has been developed since 1950, a period during which the rest of trade theory has fallen under the powerful unifying influence of the general-equilibrium approach developed by Heckscher, Ohlin, Lerner and Samuelson.

No doubt part of the explanation lies in the intricacy of the subject. The implications of preferential or discriminatory tariffs and taxes are much more difficult to unravel than those of non-preferential tariffs and taxes. And the associated welfare analysis, concerned as it is with the comparison of alternative 'second best' equilibria, can be quite elusive.

The subject is intricate; but it is not impossibly so. My chief purpose indeed is to show that the positive and normative problems posed by preferential trading and investing arrangements can be approached by standard general-equilibrium methods and to suggest that not all important questions need be shrugged off in the belief that 'anything can happen'.

Of course, one must make assumptions, and it is essential that they be made clear. Throughout everything that follows, then, it

is assumed that the world is stationary and that trade and investment are conducted in barter terms. Each assumption blocks or
obscures our view of important problems. But the remaining
problems are important – and one can always look forward to
'the next time'.

Most of the professional literature on preferential trading arrangements is exceedingly dull. The explanation lies in the multitude of
'cases' which must be examined if the treatment is to be complete.
Fortunately it is no longer necessary – or even polite – to be
comprehensive. In most chapters, therefore, I have been content
to merely illustrate how a question can be handled, restricting
detailed calculation to one or two important cases.

The book has a splendidly idiosyncratic structure. After the first,
chapters run in pairs, in the even members of which capital is
assumed to be internationally immobile and in the odd members
of which the same topic is treated on the assumption that capital
is mobile. 'Without loss of continuity', therefore, the reader may
consult every other chapter; indeed such a strategy may well
'maximize continuity'. For once the reader may yield to temptation
fearlessly and without remorse.

I have said some unpleasant things about the literature. It is
therefore comforting to be able to express one's indebtedness to
two superb pieces of pure theory. Jaroslav Vanek's book [9] is still
the only comprehensive treatment of free trade associations and
customs unions from the general equilibrium point of view. It is
not flawless – if it had been, I should not have thought of writing
this book: but it is path-breaking, first reading for anyone planning
to work in the field. Takashi Negishi's essay [8] on optimal preferential trading arrangements is equally original and supplements
Vanek's treatment nicely. It has provided most of the ideas for
my ch. 8.

The manuscript was prepared during a succession of short visits
in 1968 and 1969 to the Institute for International Economic
Studies, University of Stockholm. To the Director of the Institute,
Professor Ingvar Svennilson, and to its Research Secretary, Mr.
Östen Johansson, go my thanks for a thousand instinctive kind-

nesses which they will have forgotten or not even noticed. My visits to the Institute were financed in part by the Wenner-Gren Foundation.

MURRAY C. KEMP

Contents

Glossary of symbols

p_i world price of the ith commodity, in terms of a common international currency

p world price of the second commodity in terms of the first

p_i^r price of the ith commodity in country r, in terms of a common international currency

p^r price of the second commodity in terms of the first in the rth country

τ_i^r nondiscriminatory *ad valorem* rate of duty imposed by the rth country on its imports of the ith commodity

τ_i^{r*} nondiscriminatory *ad valorem* rate of duty imposed by the rth country on its exports of the ith commodity

t^r nondiscriminatory rate of tax imposed by the rth country on the earnings of foreign capital invested in the rth country

t^{r*} nondiscriminatory rate of tax imposed by the rth country on the foreign earnings of residents of the rth country

τ_i^{sr} *ad valorem* rate of duty imposed by the rth country on imports of the ith country from the sth country

τ_i^{sr*} *ad valorem* rate of duty imposed by the rth country on exports of the ith commodity to the sth country

K^r net indebtedness of the rth country, in the natural units of capital

M_i^r marginal product of capital in the ith industry in the rth country

m_i^s marginal propensity to buy the ith good in the sth country

s_i^j one plus the rate of tax imposed by the jth country on its consumption of the ith commodity

CHAPTER 1

Introduction

This introductory chapter contains a lexicon of terms and a description of some key price relationships which must be satisfied in any international equilibrium and which form a foundation for nearly all later calculation. These relationships are easy to trip over and are less well known than they deserve to be; they are therefore described in detail and in rather greater generality than is necessary for our purposes.

1.1. Equilibrium price relationships

1.1.1. Free trade

Suppose that n countries trade freely in m commodities, that each country absorbs some of each commodity, and that prices are quoted in terms of a common international unit of account. Let p_i^r be the price of the ith commodity in country r. Then, in market equilibrium,

$$p_i^r = p_i^s \qquad\qquad r,s = 1, ..., n; i = 1, ..., m. \quad (1.1)$$

That is, for each commodity the same price prevails everywhere.

1.1.2. Nondiscriminatory tariff-ridden trade, free of quantitative restrictions

If the assumption of free trade is relaxed the conditions of equilibrium assume a more complicated form. Suppose first that the rth country is free to tax both its imports and its exports of each commodity but must refrain from discriminating between countries; that its imports of the ith commodity are taxed at the nondiscriminatory *ad valorem* rate of $100\tau_i^r$ per cent; and that its exports of the same commodity are taxed at the nondiscriminatory *ad valorem* rate of $100\tau_i^{r*}$ per cent; with the import duty applied to the foreign price and the export duty applied to the domestic price. For the time being no restrictions are placed on the signs of τ_i^r and τ_i^{r*}; however, we do rule out subsidies of 100 per cent and above. Now in market equilibrium and in the absence of direct import controls the domestic price cannot exceed the foreign price corrected for the import duty:

$$p_i^r \leqslant p_i^s(1 + \tau_i^r) \qquad s = 1, ..., n; i = 1, ..., m. \quad (1.2a)$$

(If the inequality were not satisfied, traders would have an incentive to expand the rth country's imports.) Of course the weak inequality becomes an equality if the rth country's gross imports from the sth country are positive. Similarly, in equilibrium and in the absence of direct controls over exports, the foreign price cannot exceed the domestic price corrected for the export duty:

$$p_i^r(1 + \tau_i^{r*}) \geqslant p_i^s \qquad s = 1, ..., n; i = 1, ..., n. \quad (1.2b)$$

(If the inequality were not satisfied, traders would have an incentive to expand the rth country's exports.) Of course the weak inequality becomes an equality if the rth country's gross exports to the sth country are positive.

In stating the conditions of equilibrium in this way we free ourselves of the necessity of pretending that we know in advance whether a country is a net debtor or a net creditor. The debtor-creditor status of each country is determined by the market and we, economist-observers interested only in writing down equilibrium conditions general enough to cover all possible outcomes, do not need to know what the market decides.

Combining inequalities (1.2a) and (1.2b) we find that, in market equilibrium and in the absence of direct controls, the import and export duties imposed on any particular commodity must satisfy the further inequality

$$(1 + \tau_i^r)(1 + \tau_i^{r*}) \geq 1. \tag{1.3}$$

It follows that at most one rate of duty may be negative and that if either rate of duty is zero the other must be nonnegative. If (1.3) is satisfied as a strict inequality, trade in the ith good must be in one direction only, that is, gross and net imports must be equal.

The equilibrium conditions (1.2a) and (1.2b) apply equally to trade in finished goods and to trade in factor services. Suppose that the rth country borrows from and/or lends to the sth country, with capital defined as a homogeneous physical stock. Equivalently, we may view the rth country as importing and/or exporting the services of capital. One then has only to identify capital services with the jth good to find a place for them in the preceding analysis. If instead of an import and an export duty one wishes to apply a tax (at rate $100t^r$ per cent) on the earnings of foreign capital invested in country r and a tax (at rate $100t^{r*}$ per cent) on the earnings of domestic capital invested abroad, one has only to apply a simple transformation. Instead of conditions (1.2a) and (1.2b) we have

$$p_j^r(1 - t^r) \leq p_j^s \tag{1.4a}$$

and

$$p_j^r \geq p_j^s(1 - t^{r*})$$

respectively, with $t^r = \tau_j^r/(1 + \tau_j^r)$ and $t^{r*} = \tau_j^{r*}/(1 + \tau_j^{r*})$. And instead of inequality (1.3) we have[1])

$$(1 - t^r)(1 - t^{r*}) \leq 1. \tag{1.5}$$

1.1.3. Three conventions

In later chapters it will be found convenient to 'normalize' each country's tariff structure by supposing that imports are taxed only if net imports are positive and that exports are taxed only if net exports are positive. Given this convention, it follows from inequality (1.3) that in the absence of quantitative controls over trade all rates of duty are non-negative.

A second convention will be useful. Suppose that the rth country is either a net importer of the ith commodity from country s or a net exporter of the ith commodity to country s. Then at least one of the weak inequalities (1.2a) and (1.2b) must be satisfied as an equality. Given the normalizing convention just described, either

$$p_i^r = p_i^s(1 + \tau_i^r) \qquad\qquad \tau_i^r \geqslant 0, \quad \tau_i^{r*} = 0 \qquad\qquad (1.6a)$$

or

$$p_i^r(1 + \tau_i^{r*}) = p_i^s \qquad\qquad \tau_i^{r*} \geqslant 0, \quad \tau_i^r = 0. \qquad\qquad (1.6b)$$

Suppose however that we define the export duty as applicable not to the domestic price but to the foreign price. Then clearly it suffices to write the single equilibrium condition (1.6a), it being understood that τ_i^r is an import duty if net imports are positive and an export duty if net exports are positive and that if τ_i^r is an export duty it is applied to the foreign price. Defined as applicable to the domestic price, the rate of export duty τ_i^{r*} may be calculated from the relation

$$(1 + \tau_i^{r*})(1 + \tau_i^r) = 1$$

whence

$$\tau_i^{r*} = -\tau_i^r/(1 + \tau_i^r). \qquad\qquad (1.7)$$

Suppose that the tariff structure of country r is normalized. Even so, any feasible pattern of trade can be attained by manipulating just $(m - 1)$ rates of duty. As a third convention, then, one tariff will be equated to zero.

1.1.4. Discriminatory tariff-ridden trade, free of quantitative restrictions

The equilibrium conditions (1.2) can be generalized in several directions. First we note the possibility that the rth country discriminates between its trading partners, differentiating its import and export duties according to source and destination. Let τ_i^{sr} be the rate of duty imposed by country r on imports of the ith commodity from country s, and let τ_i^{rs} be the rate of duty imposed by country r on exports of the ith commodity to country s. The generalized conditions are then

$$p_i^r \leqslant p_i^s(1 + \tau_i^{sr}) \tag{1.8a}$$

and

$$p_i^r(1 + \tau_i^{rs*}) \geqslant p_i^s \tag{1.8b}$$

whence

$$(1 + \tau_i^{sr})(1 + \tau_i^{rs*}) \geqslant 1. \tag{1.9}$$

Alternatively, we may suppose that not only country r but every country imposes import and export duties. If import duties are imposed on the tax-free foreign price, the relevant conditions are

$$p_i^r \leqslant p_i^s(1 + \tau_i^{s*})(1 + \tau_i^r) \tag{1.10a}$$

and

$$p_i^r(1 + \tau_i^{r*})(1 + \tau_i^s) \geqslant p_i^s \tag{1.10b}$$

whence

$$(1 + \tau_i^r)(1 + \tau_i^{r*})(1 + \tau_i^s)(1 + \tau_i^{s*}) \geqslant 1. \tag{1.11}$$

If discrimination by country is possible, the conditions become

$$p_i^r \leqslant p_i^s(1 + \tau_i^{sr*})(1 + \tau_i^{sr}) \tag{1.12a}$$

and

$$p_i^r(1 + \tau_i^{rs*})(1 + \tau_i^{rs}) \geqslant p_i^s \tag{1.12b}$$

whence

$$(1 + \tau_i^{rs})(1 + \tau_i^{rs*})(1 + \tau_i^{sr})(1 + \tau_i^{sr*}) \geqslant 1. \tag{1.13}$$

Applying the first two conventions of the preceding subsection, inequalities (1.8), (1.10) and (1.12) reduce to

$$p_i^r = p_i^s(1 + \tau_i^{sr}) \tag{1.14}$$

$$p_i^r(1 + \tau_i^s) = p_i^s(1 + \tau_i^r) \tag{1.15}$$

and

$$p_i^r(1 + \tau_i^{rs}) = p_i^s(1 + \tau_i^{sr}) \tag{1.16}$$

respectively.

1.1.5. Trade subject to quantitative restrictions

The above equilibrium conditions presuppose the absence of quantitative restrictions on trade. Thus if exports are banned conditions (1.2b) and (1.3) need not be satisfied in equilibrium. It is quite possible, for example, for a country to subsidize imports ($\tau_i^r < 0$) and yet impose no offsetting tax on exports; the ban on exports serves the same purpose as a prohibitive export duty.

1.2. Definitions

Two or more countries form a *trading club* if they exchange small tariff preferences on all goods other than the services of capital. The proportion in which duties are reduced is the same for all goods[2]) and for all members and is sufficiently small that, separately and collectively, members export (import) the same commodities before and after the agreement.

The effective exchange of trade preferences involves more than the reciprocal lowering of duties by club members. Thus suppose that initially, before the formation of the club, country r imports commodity i both from country s and from country z, that the entry of commodity i into country s is unimpeded, and that r and s (but not z) join the club. Clearly the preferential character of the tariff cuts will be lost if z can ship its goods to r through s, paying only the lower duty at the r-s border. To make the preferences effective, either s must impose a transit tax or import duty on z's goods or r must tax according to the ultimate origin of its imports.

Two or more countries form an *investing club* if they exchange small tariff (or tax) preferences on the services of capital. The proportion in which duties (or taxes) are reduced is the same for all members and is sufficiently small to leave undisturbed the general pattern of international indebtedness.

Two or more countries form a *free trade association* if they abolish duties on their mutual trade in all goods other than the services of capital.

Two or more countries form a *customs union* if they form a free trade association and, in addition, adopt a common schedule of tariffs on trade (in goods other than the services of capital) with the rest of the world.

1.3. The cast

The equilibrium relationships of section 1.1 and the definitions of section 1.2 have been stated in some generality. To properly pose the problems associated with preferential trading and investing arrangements, however, one need recognize only three trading countries and two traded commodities (other than the services of capital). The remainder of the performance will be given by this skeleton cast.

NOTES

[1]) To emphasize the complete parallelism between the treatment of trade in final goods and trade in factor services, we note that, just as a suitable tax on the earnings of capital has the same effect as a tariff on trade in capital services, so a suitable tax on the proceeds of trade in final goods has the same effect as a conventional tariff. Simple transformations similar to those provided in the text are available.

[2]) We shall throughout employ a neoclassical model of production, with produced raw materials ignored. For such a model the rate of import duty imposed on a particular commodity and the rate of protection afforded the industry producing that commodity are the same. We therefore may speak interchangeably of the rate of duty and the rate of protection. In more general models, with produced raw materials admitted, this is not so. A tariff imposed on a raw material obviously affords negative protection to the industry using the raw material; less obviously, the tariff affords negative protection to any industry using the nontraded product of the domestic industry using the imported raw material; and so on. To calculate the net degree of protection afforded a particular industry, it is necessary to undertake a complicated calculation involving potentially the entire tariff schedule. The calculation of the changes in the schedule which produce equiproportionate changes in rates of effective protection is similarly complicated. To illustrate, we examine the very special case in which technology is of the no-joint-products, fixed-coefficients type and the same everywhere, in which world prices are fixed, and in which all goods are traded.

Let a_{ij} be the amount of the ith product needed to produce a unit of the jth, with units chosen so that all world prices are unity. The value added by the jth industry in any free-trading country which produces the jth commodity is then

$$v_j = 1 - \sum_i a_{ij}$$

and the value added in any tariff-ridden country r is

$$v_j^r = 1 + \tau_j^r - \sum_i a_{ij} (1 + \tau_i^r).$$

The effective rate of protection of the jth industry, $\pi_j{}^r$, is then defined by

$$v_j^r = (1 + \pi_j^r)v_j.$$

It follows that

$$\pi_j^r = (v_j^r/v_j) - 1$$
$$= (\tau_j^r - \sum_i a_{ij} \tau_i^r)/v_j$$

so that

$$d\pi_j^r = (d\tau_j^r - \sum_i a_{ij}\, d\tau_i^r)/v_j$$

and

$$d\pi_j^r/(1 + \pi_j^r) = (d\tau_j^r - \sum_i a_{ij}\, d\tau_j^r)/v_j^r.$$

If all effective rates of protection are to change in the same proportion, the left-hand side of this expression must be the same for all j. Thus, switching to matrix notation

$$\alpha v^r = (I - a)d\tau^r$$

where $\alpha \equiv d\tau_j^r/(1 + \pi_j^r)$, $a \equiv (a_{ij})$ and I is the unit matrix. It follows that the required changes in the tariff schedule are given by

$$d\tau^r = \alpha(I - a)^{-1}v^r.$$

In the special case in which there are no produced raw materials, $a = 0$, $v_j = 1$ and $v_j^r = 1 + \tau_j^r$. Hence $d\tau_j^r = \alpha(1 + \tau_j^r)$ and rates of duty and protection coincide.

For a more complete discussion of the concept of effective protection, see Corden [2].

CHAPTER 2

Preferential trading and investing clubs 1

Three countries, labelled A, B and C, trade in two commodities. Initially each country levies an import duty the proceeds of which are distributed in lump-sum fashion to its residents. The international indebtedness of each country is zero.

The initial equilibrium is disturbed when A and B form a preferential trading club. What are the implications for the pattern of world trade, for the welfare of each member country, for the welfare of the club members collectively, and for the welfare of the rest of the trading world?

Any change in a country's tariff structure is likely to harm some people and benefit others, both at home and in other trading countries. To pose our questions about welfare without engaging in interpersonal utility comparisons, therefore, it is necessary to suppose that contrary movements of individual welfare within each country are discretely annulled by lump-sum redistributions of income. These background transfers enable us to draw consistent families of Scitovsky and trade indifference curves and to deduce from them both collective behaviour and changes in communal welfare.

Two cases may be distinguished, according as A and B export the same or different commodities. In the former case a club would be totally ineffective, changing nothing of interest. We therefore focus our attention on the alternative possibility; specifically, we suppose that initially, before the establishment of the club, A exports the second commodity, B the first, and that collectively the two countries export the second commodity.

2.1. Constant terms of trade

The initial trading equilibrium may be given a simple graphical representation. Consider fig. 2.1, which contains a family of trade indifference curves for country A. If the country trades freely and is confronted with world terms of trade indicated by the slope of the line TOT, it will export OG of the first commodity and import OH of the second. If the terms of trade improve to a point indicated by T'OT', the exported and imported commodities will interchange:

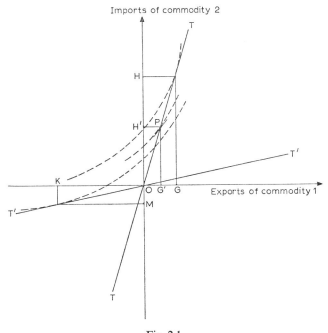

Fig. 2.1.

OK of the first commodity will be imported and OM of the second exported. Our interest, however, lies not in free trade but in tariff-ridden trade. Suppose again that the world terms of trade are represented by TOT but imagine now that the first commodity is subject to a positive import duty. Evidently the duty raises the domestic price of the first commodity above the world level. To find the new trading equilibrium therefore it is necessary to search along TOT for a point at which the intersecting trade indifference curve has the appropriate slope. By assumption, such a point exists; and, from the concavity of the welfare function, it

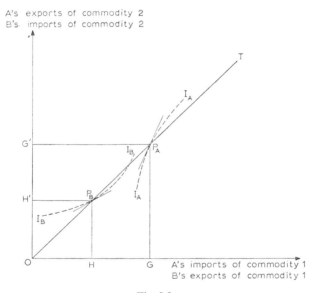

Fig. 2.2.

must lie to the left of the free-trade equilibrium. Indeed there may be many such points. In fig. 2.1 point *P* represents a possible new equilibrium, with OG′ of the first commodity exported and OH′ of the second imported.

In similar fashion country B's initial equilibrium may be represented in the third quadrant by a point on TOT where the intersecting indifference curve has a slope proportional to B's internal price ratio. To display the initial world trading equilibrium compactly, the third quadrant is now rotated through 180° and superimposed on the first. The result, much simplified, is fig. 2.2. At the terms of trade indicated by OT, A imports OG of the first commodity and pays for it with OG′ of the second commodity; country B, on the other hand, imports OH′ of the second commodity and exports OH of the first. Jointly, A and B export G′H′ of the second commodity in return for GH of the first. $P_A P_B$ is therefore the initial joint trading vector of A and B.

The initial trading equilibrium displayed in fig. 2.2 is disturbed by the establishment by A and B of a preferential trading club. We seek now to depict the new equilibrium. Throughout the present section it will be assumed that A and B are so small that the formation of the club has only a negligible effect on the world terms of trade, that is, the terms on which C buys and sells.

On forming the club A and B reciprocally lower their import duties. In B the relative price of the second commodity falls. Hence if B is incompletely specialized in production its output of the first commodity increases and its output of the second commodity declines; and if B is already completely specialized in producing for export output remains unchanged. But the tariff concessions are infinitesimal; whatever the pattern of production in B, therefore, the change in B's export supply also must be infinitesimal. It follows that country A must continue to draw from C part of its supply of the first commodity. Since both C's prices and the duties imposed by A on its trade with C are unchanged, so must be A's internal prices. Hence, finally, whatever the pattern of its production A's outputs will not be affected by the exchange of preferences.

We may from these observations deduce the implications of the tariff concessions for the welfare of each member country. Since A's duties on its trade with B have been reduced, without any offsetting changes in A's internal prices, B's terms of trade must improve. B's new trading opportunity line may be represented therefore by the line OT_B in fig. 2.3a.[1]) B's internal price ratio also must move in favour of the first commodity. B's new equilibrium may be represented therefore by the point $P_B′$ on OT_B where the intersecting trade indifference curve has the slope of the new price line. Let $E_B′ E_B′$ be the B-Engel curve associated with the new B-prices. Then $P_B′$ lies at the intersection of $E_B′ E_B′$ and OT_B. In the absence of inferiority in consumption, the Engel curve passes to the right of P_B and defines a preferred new equilibrium at P'_B. The same is true when the second or imported commodity is inferior. It is true even when the first or exported commodity is inferior provided the

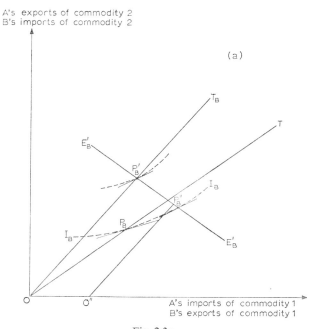

Fig. 2.3a.

inferiority is not too marked. The critical degree of inferiority is registered when $E'_B E'_B$ and OT_B are parallel, that is, when B's marginal propensity to buy the export good is equal to the reciprocal of one minus the product of (one plus the rate of import duty) and (one plus the rate of export duty).[2])

For A the only immediate effect of the exchange of preferences is a deterioration of the terms on which it trades with B. (The terms on which A trades with C are, of course, unchanged.) It follows that, strong inferiority aside, A's welfare must deteriorate. Consider fig. 2.3b. After the exchange of preferences the locus of A's trading opportunities is the jointed line $OP'_B T_A$. All of B's trade is with A, hence P'_B is the appropriate origin for A's trade with the rest of the world. From P'_B A trades, at the constant world terms of trade, to P'_A where the intersecting trade indifference curve has a slope proportional to A's constant internal price ratio. Let $E_A E_A$ be the A-Engel curve associated with A's internal prices. Then P'_A lies at the intersection of $E_A E_A$ and $P'_B T_A$. In the absence of inferiority, the Engel curve defines a new equilibrium at P'_A with everyone

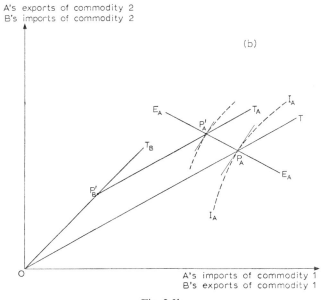

Fig. 2.3b

worse off. This is still so if the first or imported commodity is inferior. It is true even if the second or exported commodity is inferior, provided the inferiority is not too severe. The critical degree of severity is registered when $E_A E_A$ and OT are parallel at P_A, that is, when A's marginal propensity to buy its export good is equal to the reciprocal of the product of (one plus the rate of import duty) and (one plus the rate of export duty).[3])

The joint trade of the two club members is indicated by the vector $P'_A P'_B$. The latter may exceed $P_A P_B$, in which case the exchange of preferences by A and B may be said to have *created* trade with the rest of the world; or it may fall short of $P_A P_B$, in which case the exchange of preferences may be said to have *diverted* trade.[4]) The precise outcome depends on the curvature at P_B of B's initial indifference curve $I_B I_B$ and on the relative slopes of the two Engel curves.

So far we have established the following propositions. *Strong inferiority aside, the creation of the preferential trading club operates to the advantage of whichever member trades only with the other member, and operates to the disadvantage of the latter. The joint trade of the two club members with the rest of the world may either expand* (trade creation) *or contract* (trade diversion).

Since one benefits and the other suffers from the exchange of preferences, it is not possible to assert that collectively the club members are better off or worse off than before the exchange of preferences. However it is easy to see that, inferiority aside, *B could overcompensate A for its loss and yet remain better off than in the initial equilibrium*. Thus suppose B were to make a lump payment to A of an amount OO'' of the first commodity (see fig. 2.3a). B then would move to P''_B along the trading line $O'' P''_B$, which is drawn parallel to OP'_B. At P''_B B is better off than at P_B. A would then move from P''_B along a trading line parallel to OT to a point preferred to P_A. A similar conclusion is available even in the face of strong inferiority. This is a striking conclusion which does not immediately appeal to one's intuition. The common sense may be found in the fact that B's internal price ratio has moved closer both to A's price ratio and to the world price ratio. The narrowing of the two price differentials results in more efficient (strictly, not less efficient) production within the club and widens the scope for mutually beneficial (compensated) trade.

2.2. Variable terms of trade

The assumption that world prices are constant has helped us get our bearings. Now it must be relaxed and our conclusions re-examined.

Suppose first that at constant world prices the exchange of tariff preferences would give rise to trade *creation*. If in fact world prices are variable they must move in favour of the first commodity. Strong inferiority aside, the price change operates to the advantage

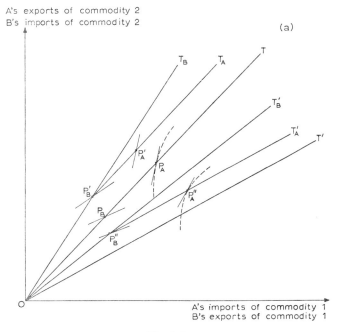

Fig. 2.4a

of B and to the disadvantage of A. Hence our earlier conclusion – that A will suffer, B benefit, from the exchange of preferences – is simply reinforced.

In the case of trade *diversion* the analysis is more intricate, even when the complications arising from strong inferiority are ignored. We concluded in section 2.1 that, in this case also, A must suffer and B benefit. Trade diversion, however, implies that if the terms of trade are sensitive to changes in demand they must improve; and this suggests the possibility that A may gain and/or B lose. Consider fig. 2.4a. The new world price ratio is indicated by the slope of OT′ and B's new terms of trade by the slope of OT′$_B$.[5]) The new B-equilibrium is indicated by P''_B, where the slope of the intersecting trade indifference curve is equal to the new internal price ratio.[6]) A then trades (with C) from P''_B to P''_A at the new world

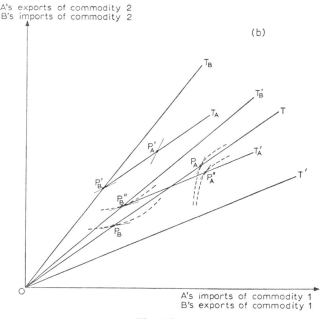

Fig. 2.4b.

price ratio. Clearly A benefits from association and B loses, so that our earlier conclusions are turned upside down: the member harmed by the exchange of preferences is now the member which in the final equilibrium trades only with the other member. Of course,

such a radical revision of our earlier conclusions requires a substantial rate of improvement in the world price of the second
commodity (though it is not necessary that foreign import demand
be inelastic). More modest changes in the terms of trade are
associated with less sweeping changes in our earlier conclusions.
It is possible, indeed, that those conclusions – that A suffers, B
benefits from the exchange of preferences – emerge unscathed.
It is also possible for both members to benefit (as fig. 2.4b shows).
It is not possible, however, for both to suffer. To sum up: in the
event of trade diversion at the initial world prices, and putting
aside the possibility of strong inferiority, at least one country will
benefit from the exchange of preferences; either member may
benefit, either may suffer.

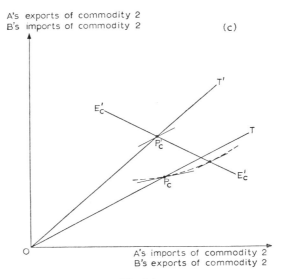

Fig. 2.4c.

Thus our conclusions for the general case in which world prices
are variable may be summarized as follows. *Strong inferiority aside,
the exchange of trade preferences by A and B may result in either
the creation or the diversion of their joint trade with the rest of the*

world. At least one member must benefit from club membership. If the exchange of preferences results in trade creation, that member which trades only within the club must benefit, the other member must suffer. If the exchange of preferences results in trade diversion, either member or both may benefit.

When world prices are variable the rest of the world is not indifferent to the exchange of preferences by A and B. However the relationship between C's welfare and its terms of trade is not quite straightforward. It is tempting to assert that C's welfare must improve if its terms of trade improve. This simple relationship does indeed hold if C is a free-trading country. It also holds if inferiority is absent or confined to the imported commodity (see fig. 2.4c). If however the exported commodity is sufficiently inferior an improvement in C's terms of trade may give rise to a loss of welfare. The critical degree of inferiority is registered when the C-Engel curve defined by C's new internal prices is parallel to its terms of trade line, that is, when the marginal propensity to buy its export good is equal to the reciprocal of the product of (one plus the rate of import duty) and (one plus the rate of export duty).[7] It will be shown in section 2.2, however, that for this paradoxical outcome it is necessary that more than one C-equilibrium be possible at the initial terms of trade and that the actual equilibrium P_C be inferior to alternative equilibria.

NOTES

[1] Throughout chs. 2 and 3 we are concerned with small (strictly, infinitesimal) changes in the rate of duty and other quantities. In the diagrams, however, it is necessary to exaggerate the changes.

[2] The slope of the curve $E_B'E_B'$ is approximately

$$-(1/p^B)(m_2^B/m_1^B) = -(1/p^B)[(1 - m_1^B)/m_1^B]$$

where m_i^B is B's marginal propensity to buy the ith commodity and p^B is the relative price in B of the second commodity in terms of the first. The slope of OT_B, on the other hand, is approximately $(1/p)$, where p is the relative world price of the second commodity in terms of the first. In equilibrium, however,

$$p^B = p(1 + \tau_2^B)/(1 + \tau_1^B).$$

Hence the two curves are parallel if

$$m_1^B = 1/[1 - (1 + \tau_2^B)/(1 + \tau_1^B)]$$

that is, recalling the conventions of section 1.1, if

$$m_1^B = 1/[1 - (1 + \tau_1^{B*})(1 + \tau_2^B)].$$

3) The slope of the curve $E_A E_A$ is

$$-(1/p^A)(m_2^A/m_1^A) = -(1/p^A)[m_2^A/(1 - m_2^A)]$$

where m_i^A is A's marginal propensity to buy the ith commodity and p^A is the relative price in A of the second commodity in terms of the first. The slope of OT, on the other hand, is $(1/p)$. In equilibrium, however,

$$p^A(1 + \tau_1^A)/(1 + \tau_2^A) = p.$$

Hence the two curves are parallel if

$$m_2^A = 1/[1 - (1 + \tau_1^A)/(1 + \tau_2^A)]$$

that is, recalling the conventions of section 1.1, if

$$m_2^A = 1/[1 - (1 + \tau_1^A)(1 + \tau_2^{A*})].$$

4) The terms *trade creation* and *trade diversion* were introduced by Viner in his pioneering study of 1950 ([10], p. 44). Since then they have been common currency in the exchange of ideas. The reader is warned therefore that the terms are here used in senses very different from Viner's.

5) Notice that in drawing fig. 2.4a it has been assumed that B's terms of trade have deteriorated. A necessary and sufficient condition for this outcome is easy to calculate. B's initial terms of trade are, of course, $(p_1/p_2) = (1/p)$. Its new terms of trade, on the other hand, are

$$\frac{(p_1 + dp_1)(1 + \tau_1^A)/(1 + \tau_1^A + d\tau_1^A)}{(p_2 + dp_2)(1 + \tau_2^A)/(1 + \tau_2^A + d\tau_2^A)} = \frac{[1 + d\tau_2^A/(1 + \tau_2^A)]}{p[1 + (dp/p)][1 + d\tau_1^A/(1 + \tau_1^A)]}$$

where $d\tau_1^A$ and $d\tau_2^A$ apply to A's trade with B only. Alternatively, referring to the conventions of section 1.1, the new terms of trade may be written

$$\frac{(p_1 + dp_1)(1 + \tau_1^A)/(1 + \tau_1^A + d\tau_1^A)}{(p_2 + dp_2)(1 + \tau_2^{A*} + d\tau_2^{A*})/(1 + \tau_2^{A*})} =$$

$$= \{p[1 + (dp/p)][1 + d\tau_1^A/(1 + \tau_1^A)][1 + d\tau_2^{A*}/(1 + \tau_2^{A*})]\}^{-1}.$$

Thus the terms of trade improve or deteriorate as the product of one plus the proportionate change in the world price ratio, one plus the proportionate change in the import duty, and one plus the (properly defined) proportionate change in the export duty is less than or greater than zero.

[6]) In drawing fig. 2.4a it has been assumed that B's internal price ratio has moved in favour of the second or imported commodity. A necessary and sufficient condition for this outcome may be obtained as follows. Initially, B's internal price ratio is

$$p^B = p_2^B/p_1^B = p(1 + \tau_2^B)/(1 + \tau_1^B)$$

$$= p(1 + \tau_2^B)(1 + \tau_1^{B*}).$$

In the new equilibrium, the internal price ratio is $(1 + \tau_2{}^B + d\tau_2{}^B)(1 + \tau_1{}^{B*} + d\tau_1{}^{B*})$ times (the inverse of) the new terms of trade given in the preceding note; that is, it is

$$p^B\left(1 + \frac{dp}{p}\right)\left[1 + \frac{d\tau_1^A}{1 + \tau_1^A}\right]\left[1 + \frac{d\tau_2^{A*}}{1 + \tau_2^{A*}}\right]$$

$$\left[1 + \frac{d\tau_2^B}{1 + \tau_2^B}\right]\left[1 + \frac{d\tau_1^{B*}}{1 + \tau_1^{B*}}\right].$$

By assumption, however, the square-bracketed terms are equal to each other and less than unity. Thus the internal price ratio in B is

$$bp^B\left(1 + \frac{dp}{p}\right) \qquad 0 < b < 1.$$

It is therefore greater or less than the initial price ratio as $b[1 + (dp/p)]$ is greater or less than unity.

[7]) The proof follows the same lines as in notes 2 and 3.

CHAPTER 3

Preferential trading and investing clubs II

Throughout ch. 2 we adopted the classical assumption that factors of production are internationally immobile. The convenience of the assumption is great. In particular it has enabled us to study the response of each country separately to a change in world prices. When the assumption is abandoned one must recognize that changes in commodity prices entail changes in factor rewards in all countries and therefore give rise to equilibrating movements of factors between countries. The extent of the movements depends on conditions of demand and supply in all trading countries. Hence it is impossible to calculate the implications of a price change for one country without considering the implications for all countries.

In the present chapter we consider the implications of preferential trading and investing clubs on the revised assumption that capital is internationally mobile and distributes itself between the three trading countries in whatever manner will equalize returns after tax for the lending country. Alternatively, we might have extended the analysis to embrace international labour mobility. Quantitatively, however, labour mobility is less important than capital mobility. Moreover, welfare assessments in the face of changing populations are notoriously difficult. We will continue to assume therefore that internationally labour is completely immobile.

The least troublesome way of accommodating capital movements is simply to identify with the services of capital one of the two traded goods recognized in ch. 2. For coping with some questions the analysis of ch. 2, reinterpreted in this way, would suffice. It would preserve the distinction between goods flows and factor flows and thus enable us to distinguish between trade preferences and investment preferences. And it is exceedingly simple. However it would have the major weakness of implying that there is in each country just one produced commodity, the same commodity in each country. Thus trade, in the narrow sense of exchange of one produced good for another, would be ruled out. Of course it would be possible to overcome the latter objection by imagining that each country produces a different commodity, but that would introduce an undesirable element of asymmetry and, in any case, would take us *away* from the model of ch. 2.

For these reasons I have decided to retain the assumption that, potentially at least, each of the three countries produces two commodities. The purpose of the present chapter therefore is to extend the analysis of ch. 2 to accommodate three rather than two traded goods – the original pair plus the services of capital. To emphasize the formal continuity of the analysis in these two chapters it might now be assumed that trade in capital services is dutiable. Instead, convention is upheld and it is supposed that the reward of foreign capital is subject to an income tax; specifically, it is assumed that, if it is a net debtor, a member country levies a tax of arbitrary magnitude on the earnings of foreign capital invested within its borders and that, if it is a net creditor, a member taxes its own foreign earnings. Of course, anything a tax on earnings can do a duty could equally well do – and *vice versa*.[1])

The proceeds of all duties and taxes are assumed to be distributed in lump-sum fashion to the residents of the taxing country.

When the possibility of borrowing and lending is introduced, it must be recognized that a country may have no imports other than capital services, or it may have two imports. We therefore must generalize our earlier assumption concerning the pattern of specialization within the club. Throughout the present chapter it will be assumed that if country A (B) imports anything it imports the first (second) commodity, and that if A and B collectively import anything they import the first commodity.

For simplicity we suppose that country C is free-trading, so that C's prices can be identified with world prices; and that C levies no income taxes, so that the rate of capital rental in C may be identified with the world rate. If these assumptions are relaxed, our conclusions change only in inessential details.

An initial equilibrium is disturbed when A and B form a preferential trading club and/or a preferential investing club. What are the implications for the pattern of world trade and indebtedness, for the welfare of club members, individually and collectively, and for the welfare of the rest of the world?

3.1. Constant world prices

Following the procedure of ch. 2, we consider first the exchange of preferences by two small countries neither of which exerts an appreciable influence on world commodity prices or capital rentals. Under these assumptions, country C must be incompletely specialized in production. On the other hand, it will now be argued that, without sensible loss of generality, we may suppose that both member countries are completely specialized in production.

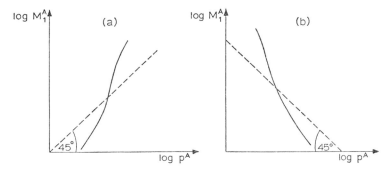

Fig. 3.1a. First commodity labour-intensive.
Fig. 3.1b. First commodity capital-intensive.

In developing the argument, and throughout the chapter, the following additional notation will be used:

K^s the net indebtedness of country s, expressed in natural units of capital ($K^s \gtrless 0$)

M_i^s the marginal product of capital in the ith industry in country s

p_i the world price of the ith commodity in terms of a common international unit of account

p the world price of the second commodity in terms of the first

p^s the relative price of the second commodity in terms of the first in country s

Consider the curves of figs. 3.1a and 3.1b. Each curve is drawn on the assumption that in country A specialization is incomplete. In conformity to the Stolper-Samuelson theorem, the slopes of the curves are greater than one in magnitude. Now as a condition of commodity market equilibrium[2])

$$p^A(1 + \tau_1^A) = p^C = p \tag{3.1a}$$

and as a condition of capital market equilibrium [3])

$$M_1^A(1 + \tau_1^A)(1 - t^A) = M_1^C. \tag{3.1b}$$

Both p and M_1^C are constants, as are τ_1^A and t^A; hence eqs. (3.1a) and (3.1b) rigidly determine p^A and M_1^A. It is conceivable, of course, that the point thus determined lies on the curve of fig. 3.1. Indeed τ_1^A and t^A may be carefully chosen to ensure that outcome. If however the rates of duty and tax are assigned random values, the probability of the point lying on the curve is zero. Throughout the present section, therefore, it is assumed that A is completely specialized in production.

For similar reasons it is assumed that B is completely specialized.

As an interesting corollary of the above analysis we note that, corresponding to each world price ratio, there is (at most) a single internal price ratio consistent with incomplete specialization. Thus when the Heckscher-Ohlin model of international trade is broadened to incorporate capital mobility it behaves like the Ricardian model it was designed to replace. The reason of course is that, within limits set by national capital endowments, there is in the extended model just one fixed factor (labour).

3.1.1. The formation of a preferential trading club

A country will not join a trading club if it is clear in advance that it cannot possibly benefit from doing so. For a country to benefit from membership it is necessary that it export to at least one other member. We assume therefore that A and B export to each other. Since we have already decided to assume that both A and B specialize in production, we are now assuming, in effect, that they specialize in the production of different commodities, A in the production of the second commodity, B in the production of the first.

On the other hand, we must assume that either A or B imports from C. For otherwise the *preferential* character of the concessions extended to each other by club members would be merely formal.[4])

In the light of these two assumptions, it will entail no further loss of generality if, as in ch. 2, it is assumed that B trades only with A whereas A trades with both B and C. It is of course possible that initially C exports to both A and B, selling the first commodity to A and the second to B. But the same final patterns of production and consumption can be achieved by channelling C's exports to B through A; and, after the exchange of preferences by A and B, C will have no incentive to export directly to B. Thus it will simplify matters, without involving any loss of essential generality, if we assume that before and after the exchange of preferences C trades only with A.

Consider the initial equilibrium of country A. If A is neither a debtor nor a creditor ($K^A = 0$), its trading opportunities are indicated by the line OT in fig. 3.2. If however A is a net debtor, its trading opportunities *after debt service* are represented by $O_A T_A$ and its initial equilibrium by P_A, where the vertical distance OO_A is equal to[5] $K^A M_2^A (1 - t^A)$, the net or after-tax earnings of foreign capital invested in A, expressed in terms of the second commodity. If on the other hand A is a net creditor, O_A lies below O by the distance $-K^A M_2^A (1 - t^A)$. In general A might then import both commodities; however such a case would be inconsistent with our assumption that A and B engage in two way trade.

Consider now the initial equilibrium of country B. If B is neither a debtor nor a creditor ($K^B = 0$), its trading opportunities are indicated by OT. If however B is a net debtor, its trading opportunities after debt service are represented by $O_B T_B$ and its initial equilibrium by P_B, where the horizontal distance OO_B is equal to[6]) $K^B M_1^B (1 - t^B)$, the net or after-tax earnings of foreign capital invested in B. If B is a net creditor, O_B lies to the left of O by the distance $-K^B M_1^B (1 - t^B)$. In the case illustrated by fig. 3.2, both A and B, and therefore the club as a whole, are net debtors. The joint exports of club members, of goods other than capital services, are indicated by WP_A and the joint imports by WP_B.

Consider next the new equilibrium of B, after an exchange of tariff preferences with A. We know from section 2.1 that the exchange of preferences will move B's internal price ratio in favour of the first or exported commodity. In the initial equilibrium B pays in debt service a (positive or negative) amount $K^B M_1^C$ in terms of the first commodity.[7]) Since M_1^C is constant, the debt service changes only if K^B changes. Thus if K^B were held constant at its initial value B's new trading possibilities would be summarized by the line $O_B T_B'$ in fig. 3.2. (In drawing fig. 3.2 it has been assumed that K^B is positive.) In fact, however, the change in B's internal price ratio raises the return to capital and gives rise to a capital inflow. The inflow may either raise or lower the total debt service. Thus in money terms the new payments are $(K^B + dK^B) M_1^C p_1$. Converting to real terms by dividing by B's new export price $p_1/[1 + d\tau_1^A/(1 + \tau_1^A)]$, we find that the new payments are $(K^B + dK^B) M_1^C [1 + d\tau_1^A/(1 + \tau_1^A)]$. The increase in payments is, therefore,

$$K^B M_1^C \left(\frac{d\tau_1^A}{1 + \tau_1^A} + \frac{dK^B}{K^B} \right). \tag{3.2}$$

If B is a net creditor this expression is necessarily positive; that is, B's receipts from foreign investments must fall. The explanation lies partly in the price-induced decline in foreign investment and partly in the decline in the profitability of both home and foreign investment. If, on the other hand, B is a net debtor expression

(3.2) may be of either sign; that is, B's payments to foreign creditors may either increase or decrease. The reason for this ambiguity is that the extent of B's indebtedness and the return to capital move in opposite directions. The precise outcome depends ultimately on the elasticity of the curve of marginal productivity in B's first industry. If expression (3.2) is negative, as it *may* be when B is a net debtor, B will benefit from the exchange of preferences: its terms of trade will have improved, the burden of its debt service will have become lighter, and its output will have increased. If (3.2) is

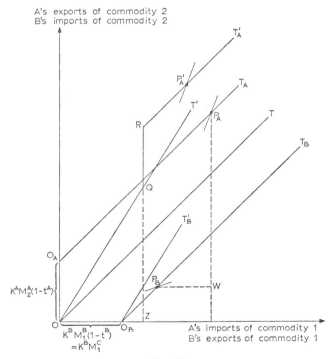

Fig. 3.2.

positive, as it *must* be when B is a net creditor, the effect on B's welfare is less obvious. We know that B's terms of trade must improve. For an improvement in B's welfare, therefore, it is sufficient (but not necessary) that A's disposable real income increase or remain constant. To obtain the change in B's disposable real income, we must subtract (3.2) from the increase in B's output. The latter is[8])

$$M_1^B dK^B = [M_1^C/(1 - t^B)]dK^B \qquad (3.3)$$

so that the net increase in B's disposable income, in terms of the first commodity, is

$$-K^B M_1^C \left(\frac{d\tau_1^A}{1 + \tau_1^A} - \frac{t^B}{1 - t^B} \frac{dK^B}{K^B} \right). \qquad (3.4)$$

Thus if B is a net debtor its disposable real income inevitably increases; and if B is a net creditor its disposable real income inevitably declines. (Remember that, if B is a net creditor, $t^B = -t^{B*}/(1 - t^{B*})$ is negative.) Strong inferiority aside, therefore, B will benefit or suffer from an exchange of preferences with A according as it is a net debtor or a net creditor, respectively.

Given the outcome for B it is possible to determine the outcome for A. We know, from section 2.1, that the exchange of tariff preferences by A and B leaves unchanged A's internal prices and, therefore, A's factor rewards and state of international indebtedness. Club membership affects A only through the deterioration of the terms on which it trades with B. It will not be found surprising, then, that, strong inferiority aside, A will be left worse off by the exchange of preferences. Consider fig. 3.2 again. In the new equilibrium B still exports the first commodity. Suppose it exports an amount OZ. All of its exports go to A on terms indicated by the slope or $O_B T_B'$ or OT'. A's origin for its trade with C, therefore, may be found by reading up from Z to say Q or OT'. A's new trading opportunity line may then be constructed by taking the jointed line $OO_A T_A$ and setting it down with its south-west extremity at Q. The new trading opportunity line, $OQRT_A'$, has two joints, at Q and R. Strong inferiority aside, the initial A-equilibrium at P_A is preferred to the new equilibrium at, say, P_A'.

It is easy to see that the joint imports of the club members may increase or decrease, and that the joint exports of the members may increase or decrease. More particularly, it is possible for both exports and imports to increase or decrease, so that we may speak unambiguously of trade creation or trade diversion. In the face of international borrowing and lending, however, it is possible for joint imports and joint exports to move in opposite directions. In that case one must be content to say that trade with the rest of the world has been neither created nor diverted.[9])

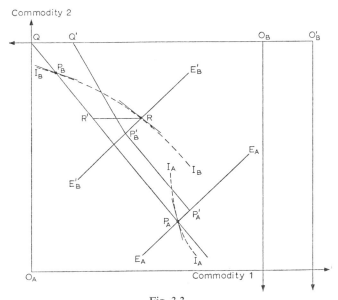

Fig. 3.3.

Subject to minor qualification, we may now reaffirm the major conclusions reached in section 2.1. *Strong inferiority aside, the creation of a preferential trading club operates to the disadvantage of whichever member maintains trading ties with the rest of the world, and operates to the advantage or disadvantage of the other member according as it is a net debtor or net creditor, respectively. These conclusions are valid regardless of the debtor-creditor status of the member which trades with the rest of the world and of the two member countries jointly. The joint trade of the two club members with the rest of the world may expand* (trade creation) *or contract* (trade diversion), *or it may do neither.*

It remains to set out the conditions under which a mutually beneficial compensated exchange of tariff preferences is possible. We show first that such an exchange is always possible if B is a net debtor. The proposition is an extremely plausible one. For we know that A's output and debt service are unchanged by club membership, that B's disposable real income increases (by the amount indicated by expression (3.4)), that the gap between the internal price ratios of the two club members narrows, and that the club as a whole is able to trade with C on unchanged terms. Nevertheless a simple diagrammatic proof may deepen our understanding and will provide a useful check that we have not omitted relevant considerations. Consider fig. 3.3, in which $I_A I_A$ and $I_B I_B$ must be interpreted as (Scitovsky) *consumption* indifference curves. Point Q, referred to the origin O_A, indicates A's initial disposable real income, that is, production corrected for debt service and expressed in terms of the second commodity. Referred to the origin O_B, Q indicates B's initial disposable real income, that is, production corrected for debt service and expressed in terms of the *first* commodity. From Q members A and B trade to P_A and P_B respectively. The exchange of tariff preferences gives rise to (i) a change in B's internal prices in favour of the first commodity and (ii) an increase in B's disposable real income from QO_B to say QO_B' and, therefore, an increase in the joint disposable real income of the two club members. Let us for a moment ignore (ii) and assume that B pays to A an amount QQ' as compensation. B then trades with A to P_B' on the improved terms indicated by the slope of $Q'P_B'$. At P_B' B is better off than at P_B. Country A trades with C from P_B' to P_A' at constant world prices. Clearly P_A' is preferred to P_A. If now we take into the reckoning the additional income $O_B O_B'$ our conclusion follows *a fortiori*. It will be obvious from the above reasoning that, even when B is a net creditor, a mutually beneficial exchange of preferences may be possible. In that case O_B' lies to the left of O_B. Provided it does not lie too far to the left, however, B can compensate A and yet derive some residual benefit from club membership. The maximum loss of real disposable income which B can sustain and still compensate A is indicated by the distance between R and R', where R is the point of intersection between $E_B'E_B'$ and the initial B-indifference curve I_BI_B and R' lies on QP_A directly to the left of R. Thus *a mutually beneficial exchange of tariff preferences is always possible if B is a net debtor; it may or may not be possible if B is a net creditor. These conclusions are independent of the debtor-creditor status of A and of the joint debtor-creditor status of A and B.*

The conclusions of this subsection generalize those of section 2.1. It will be noted that it is not true in general that the member which trades only within the club necessarily benefits from the exchange of preferences – the outcome depends crucially on the debtor-creditor status of that member. Whether a mutually beneficial exchange of preference is possible depends on the same considerations.

3.1.2. The formation of a preferential investing club

A country will not join an investing club if it is clear in advance that it cannot possibly benefit from doing so. For a country to benefit from membership it is necessary that it borrow from or lend to at least one other member. We assume therefore that initially either A is in debt to B or B is in debt to A.

On the other hand, we must assume that at least one club member borrows from or lends to C. Otherwise, the *preferential* character of the concessions extended to each other by club members would be merely formal.

In view of these two assumptions it will entail no further loss of generality if it is supposed that B has capital dealings only with A, while A deals with both B and C. Specifically, it will be assumed that either A is in debt to both B and C or A is a creditor of both B and C.

Let us consider first the case in which A is in debt to both B and C. (It follows that A and B jointly are in debt to the rest of the world.) An initial equilibrium is disturbed by the exchange of tax preferences by A and B. Consider the implications for A. In the new equilibrium A still is in debt to C, hence the real return to capital in A is the same as in the initial equilibrium. It follows that the total amount of capital at work in A, A's net indebtedness and A's total output must be unchanged. As the result of its tax concession to B, however, the burden of A's debt service increases. Thus the initial debt service is, in terms of the second commodity,[10]) $K^A M_2^A (1 - t^A)$. The new debt service is composed of two parts: payments to B, $-(K^B + dK^B)M_2^A(1 - t^A - dt^A)$, and payments to C, $(K^A + K^B + dK^B)M_2^A(1 - t^A)$. The decrease in debt service (and hence the increase in A's real disposable income) is, therefore,

$$-(K^B + dK^B)M_2^A dt^A \sim -K^B M_2^A dt^A \qquad (3.5)$$

which is negative.

For B, on the other hand, the exchange of tax preferences encourages additional foreign lending. This entails a decline in domestic output of[11])

$$-M_1^B dK^B = -M_1^C dK^B/(1 - t^B). \qquad (3.6a)$$

But it entails also an expansion of foreign earnings, for not only foreign investment but also the rate of return on that investment increases. Initially, before the formation of the club, foreign earnings, in terms of the first commodity, amount to $-K^B M_1^C$. In the new equilibrium foreign earnings are[12]) $-(K^B + dK^B)M_1^C[1 - dt^A/(1 - t^A)]$. The increase in earnings is, therefore,

$$M_1^C K^B \left(\frac{dt^A}{1 - t^A} - \frac{dK^B}{K^B} \right) \qquad (3.6b)$$

which is positive. Subtracting expression (3.6a) from (3.6b) we obtain the net increase in B's real disposable income:

$$M_1^C K^B \left(\frac{\mathrm{d}t^A}{1 - t^A} + \frac{t^B}{1 - t^B} \frac{\mathrm{d}K^B}{K^B} \right) \tag{3.7}$$

which is necessarily positive. (Recall that t^B is negative when B is a net creditor.)

We may conclude, then, that if jointly the club members are in debt to the rest of the world, the exchange of tax preferences harms the debtor-member and benefits the creditor-member.

Suppose alternatively that A is a creditor of both B and C (so that A and B jointly are creditors of C). Then, by reasoning similar to the above, or by direct analogy, we obtain expressions (3.5) and (3.7) again. This time, however, K^B and $\mathrm{d}K^B$ are both negative and $\mathrm{d}t^A$ is positive, so that the signs of (3.5) and (3.7) are reversed. We conclude, therefore, that if jointly the club members are in debt to the rest of the world the exchange of tax preferences benefits the creditor-member and either harms or benefits the debtor-member.

Summarizing the conclusions reached so far, we may say that *the exchange of tax preferences results in an unambiguous change in the real income of whichever member borrows from or lends to the rest of the world. If that member is a net creditor, it benefits; if that member is a net debtor, it suffers. The remaining member, whatever its debtor-creditor status, may benefit or suffer.*

There remains for consideration the question whether a mutually beneficial compensated exchange of tax preferences is possible. The answer is exceedingly simple: if the members are joint creditors, such an exchange is possible; if the members are joint debtors, such an exchange is impossible. To show that this is so we express the increase in A's real disposable income in terms of the first commodity and make use of the condition of capital-market equilibrium $pM_2^A(1 - t^A) = M_1^C$ to obtain $-K^B M_1^C \mathrm{d}t^A / (1 - t^A)$. Adding this expression to (3.7) we obtain the increase in the real disposable income of A and B jointly:

$$M_1^C \frac{t^B}{1 - t^B} \mathrm{d}K^B. \tag{3.8}$$

This expression has the sign of $t^B \mathrm{d}K^B$. We know that if A and B are jointly in debt $\mathrm{d}K^B$ is negative; but then $t^B = -t^{B*}/(1 - t^{B*})$ also is negative; hence $t^B \mathrm{d}K^B$ is positive. If, on the other hand, A and B are joint creditors, both t^B and $\mathrm{d}K^B$ are positive; again, therefore, $t^B \mathrm{d}K^B$ is positive. Thus *whatever the joint debtor-creditor status of club members, a mutually beneficial compensated exchange of tax preferences is always possible.*

3.1.3. The formation of preferential trading and investing clubs

Throughout this chapter we confine our attention to changes in taxes and tariffs which are infinitesimally small. This self-denial has many compensations. In particular it makes it possible to ascertain the effects of preferential trading *and investing* clubs simply by taking appropriately weighted sums of the rates of response of variables to the two types of agreement considered separately. The weights are determined by the ratio of the proportional tax concessions to the proportional tariff concessions. The implications of trading and investing clubs, at least for the most interesting case in which club members trade with and invest in each other and in which jointly they trade with and invest in the rest of the world, are therefore implicit in the two preceding subsections.

3.2. Variable world prices

We have proceeded this far on the simplifying assumption that A and B are dominated by the rest of the world. When that assumption is abandoned we are faced with two additional complications. First and obviously, we must allow for the possibility that an exchange of preferences will bring about an adjustment of world commodity prices. Second, we can no longer confine our attention to a single pattern of international specialization, with A and B completely specialized, C incompletely specialized. On the other hand, it will be argued that not all conceivable patterns of specialization need be considered.

The impact of a preferential trading or investing club depends crucially on the initial patterns of trade and indebtedness. It would be possible to examine all possible cases and catalogue all possible final outcomes; but that would require much patience – more than the objective warrants. Instead we confine ourselves to just one case – that in which A is indebted to both B and C – and consider the possible outcomes of an exchange by A and B of tax preferences. The calculations for that case will illustrate a method with which all other cases may be approached.

First, however, we seek to establish a general proposition concerning probable patterns of international specialization. It was argued in section 3.1 that, when A and B are so small that they exert only a negligible influence on world prices, it is reasonable to assume that each is completely specialized in production, and that C

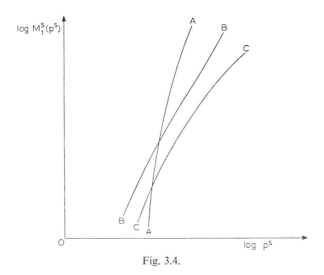

Fig. 3.4.

is incompletely specialized. It will be argued here that, when each country is large enough to appreciably influence world prices, it is reasonable to assume that at most one of them is incompletely specialized. Under the new assumption, the incompletely specialized country may be A, B or C.

In fig. 3.4 are drawn three M_1^s-curves, one for each country and without attention to endowment ratios. The figure is constructed on the assumption that in each country the second industry is relatively capital-intensive, but the argument does not hinge on that assumption. Suppose now that each country is incompletely specialized. Then, as a condition of equilibrium in the commodity markets,

$$p^A(1 + \tau_1^A) = p^B/(1 + \tau_2^B) = p \qquad (3.9a)$$

and, as a condition of equilibrium in the capital market,

$$M_1^A(1 - t^A)(1 + \tau_1^A) = M_1^B(1 - t^B) = M_1^C. \qquad (3.9b)$$

If the rates of tax and duty are sufficiently small, the first equality of eq. (3.9a) and the first equality of eq. (3.9b) together determine two points, one on the A-curve, one on the B-curve, of fig. 3.4.[13]) Similarly, the second equality of eq. (3.9a) and the second equality of eq. (3.9b) together define two points, one on the B-curve and one on the C-curve. If the rates of tax and duty are independent random variables there is zero probability that the two points on the B-curve coincide. Alternatively, bearing in mind that M_1^s is a function of p^s, we may say that there is probability zero that the four equations (3.9) in the three variables p^s are mutually consistent. We conclude that we may reasonably assume that not all countries are incompletely specialized in production.[14])

There remains for consideration the possibility that two of the three countries may be incompletely specialized. Suppose that A and B are incompletely specialized, C completely specialized. As we have just seen, given sufficiently small rates of tax and duty there exist p^A and p^B such that A and B are incompletely specialized. But is there reason to believe that the critical p^A and p^B will be established in free world markets? If we could forget about C we

might argue that, with A and B incompletely specialized, it is
within limits a matter of indifference to the owners of the world's
capital stock how that capital is allocated between countries and
that, again provided that the rates of tax and duty are small
enough, there exists an allocation which will produce the required
prices. But we cannot forget C. Only with probability zero would
the allocation of capital which generates the required domestic

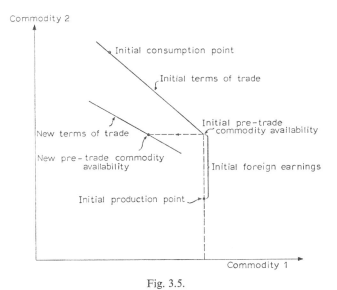

Fig. 3.5.

price ratios p^s also ensure that eq. (3.9b) is satisfied. We conclude
that it is reasonable to assume that A and/or B, as well as C, are
completely specialized. By similar arguments it can be shown that
it is reasonable to ignore the possibility that A and C or B and C
are incompletely specialized and, hence, that it is reasonable to
assume that, at most, one country is incompletely specialized.
Notice that, in arguing this proposition, it has not been necessary
to assume that production functions are everywhere the same.

With these preliminaries behind us we now consider the implications of an exchange of tax preferences by A and B. For reasons

given earlier, our attention is confined to the case in which A is in debt to B and C, with A and B jointly in debt to C. In view of the foregoing argument, we may confine our attention to just four patterns of international specialization, one in which all countries are completely specialized (A in the production of the second commodity, B and C in the production of the first) and three in which just one country is incompletely specialized. Of the latter, however, two cases (those in which, respectively, B and C are incompletely specialized) are almost completely symmetrical. It suffices therefore to consider just three cases in all.

(i) *All countries completely specialized.* Let us suppose for the time being that world prices remain constant in the face of the exchange of preferences. The immediate effect of the exchange is to make investment in A more attractive to residents of B. Capital therefore flows from B to A, raising its marginal productivity in B, lowering it in A. The flow continues until, net of tax, the two marginal returns are brought into equality. As the marginal productivity of capital falls in A, however, A becomes a less attractive avenue of investment for C. C therefore withdraws part of its capital from A, with the result that the rate of return to capital falls in C. In the new equilibrium, therefore, the marginal product of capital is lower in A and C, higher in B. Compared with the initial situation, A is a greater debtor, B a greater creditor and C a smaller creditor.

Without additional assumptions the net effect on A's welfare cannot be pinned down, even in sign. A's initial debt service, in terms of the second commodity, is

$$K^A M_2^A (1 - t^A) = -(K^B + K^C) M_2^A (1 - t^A)$$

and its new debt service is

$$-(K^B + dK^B)(M_2^A + dM_2^A)(1 - t^A - dt^A) -$$
$$- (K^C + dK^C)(M_2^A + dM_2^A)(1 - t^A)$$

where the first term represents payments to B and the second represents payments to C. The increase in A's debt service is, therefore,

$$M_2^A(1 - t^A)\left[K^B \frac{dt^A}{1 - t^A} + K^A\left(\frac{dM_2^A}{M_2^A} + \frac{dK^B}{K^B}\right)\right]$$

which may be of either sign. A's net indebtedness is greater; but its payments to C per unit of capital borrowed, and possibly its payments to B per unit of capital borrowed, are smaller. The increase in A's output, on the other hand, is

$$M_2^A dK^A > 0.$$

Hence the net increase in A's disposable real income, in terms of the second commodity, is

$$-M_2^A(1 - t^A)$$

$$\left[K^B \frac{dt^A}{1 - t^A} + K^A\left(\frac{dM_2^A}{M_2^A} - \frac{1}{1 - t^A} \cdot \frac{dK^A}{K^A} + \frac{dK^B}{K^B}\right)\right] \quad (3.10)$$

which may be of either sign. It follows that A's total demand for the first commodity may increase or decrease.

The outcome for country B is equally untidy. B's initial receipts from foreign investment are, in terms of the first commodity,

$$-K^B p M_2^A(1 - t^A) = -K^B M_1^B(1 - t^B)$$

and its new receipts are

$$-(K^B + dK^B)p(M_2^A + dM_2^A)(1 - t^A - dt^A) =$$
$$-(K^B + dK^B)(M_1^B + dM_1^B)(1 - t^B - dt^B).$$

The increase in B's receipts is, therefore,

$$-K^B M_1^B(1 - t^B)\left(-\frac{dt^B}{1 - t^B} + \frac{dM_1^B}{M_1^B} + \frac{dK^B}{K^B}\right).$$

The increase in B's output, on the other hand, is

$$M_1^B dK^B < 0$$

so that the net increase in B's disposable real income, in terms of the first commodity, is

$$-K^B M_1^B (1 - t^B) \left(\frac{dt^B}{1 - t^B} - \frac{dM_1^B}{M_1^B} + \frac{t^B}{1 - t^B} \cdot \frac{dK^B}{K^B} \right) \qquad (3.11)$$

which may be of either sign.

Only for C is the outcome clear: the rate of return on both domestic and foreign investment falls and, as a corollary, C is worse off. Without setting out the detailed accounting, we simply write down the net increase in C's real disposable income, in terms of the first commodity:[15])

$$-K^C p(1 - t^A) dM_2^A < 0.$$

While C's income falls, its output of the first commodity increases. Strong inferiority aside, therefore, C's net demand for the first commodity must fall.

Thus if world prices are undisturbed by the exchange of preferences we may be sure that only C suffers. The outcome for A and for B is undetermined. On the other hand, C's net demand for the first commodity falls but the direction of change in the net demands of A and B is uncertain. Thus the net world demand for the first commodity, and therefore the world price ratio, may move in either direction. The price change damps or magnifies the impact or constant-price effects of the exchange of preferences. To complete our account of the implications of the exchange of preferences therefore we must study the effects of a change in relative commodity prices. Suppose that the relative price of the second commodity increases. The relative profitability of investment in A increases, so that additional capital moves to A from B and C. The flow of capital depresses its marginal productivity in A, raises its marginal productivity in B and C, until the marginal return to investment is again everywhere the same. For A, therefore, the terms of trade improve; moreover, it benefits from the additional inflow of foreign capital. Thus the effect of the price change on A's welfare is unambiguous. If the impact or constant-price effects of the exchange of preferences are to A's advantage, those effects are reinforced; if the impact effects are harmful to A, the effects are damped. For the creditor countries B and C, on the other hand, the price change may be either harmful or beneficial. Both countries suffer a deterioration of the terms on which they trade; but their foreign investments are more profitable, leaving the net welfare outcome undetermined.

The foregoing discussion must be changed in obvious ways if, instead of increasing, the relative world price of the second commodity falls.

(ii) *A and B completely specialized, C incompletely specialized.* Under the assumption that world prices are constant, this case has been studied in detail in section 3.1. In A output remains unchanged, but real income declines to the extent that its debt service increases. Hence, strong inferiority aside, A's net demand for the first commodity decreases. In B output declines but foreign earnings increase; hence B's net demand for the first commodity must increase. In C real income is unchanged, while the output of the first commodity increases or decreases, according as the first industry is relatively capital-intensive or relatively labour-intensive. Hence C's net demand for the first commodity will increase or decrease, depending on the relative capital-intensities of the two industries. As in case (i), therefore, both the net demand for the first commodity and relative world prices may change in either direction. We must supplement our earlier analysis by examining the welfare implications of a change in relative commodity prices.

Suppose then that the relative price of the second commodity increases. As in case (i), this raises the return to capital in A. In the present case, however, the return to capital in C changes also. Suppose that in C the second industry is relatively capital-intensive. Then, from the Stolper-Samuelson theorem, the marginal productivity of capital increases in both industries. More specifically, the return to capital, in terms of the first commodity, increases in C in greater proportion than in A. Capital therefore flows from both A and B to C until the marginal private returns in A and B have risen to the C-level. Suppose, alternatively, that in C the second industry is relatively labour-intensive. Applying the Stolper-Samuelson theorem again, the marginal productivity of capital falls in both industries. Specifically, the return to capital, in terms of the first commodity, falls in C in greater proportion than in B. Capital therefore flows from C to both A and B until the marginal returns in A and B have *fallen* to the C-level.

The two subcases merit separate study. We consider first the subcase in which in C the second industry is relatively labour-intensive. For A the price change is unambiguously beneficial: the terms of trade improve; moreover, additional foreign capital flows in, producing a surplus on the additional capital and a reduction in the rental for the initial amount borrowed.[16]) For C, at the other extreme, the price change is unambiguously harmful, the increased purchasing power of foreign earnings only partially compensating for the adverse movement of the terms of trade and the decline in the marginal productivity of capital invested abroad.[17]) In between stands B, the outcome for which also is unfavourable. Like C, country B suffers from a deterioration of its terms of trade and from a decline in the marginal physical productivity of foreign investment. This is not offset by the decline in B's foreign investment.[18])

Turning to the second subcase, in which C's second industry is relatively capital-intensive, we find that for each country the outcome may be either favourable or unfavourable. For A the terms of trade improve, but foreign capital retreats and, on that part which remains, the real rental increases.[19]) For C the terms of trade deteriorate, but this may be more than offset by the inflow of capital and by the increased real return on the balance of its foreign investment.[20]) For B, finally, the terms of trade deteriorate but this may be more than offset by the increased return to a larger volume of foreign investment.[21])

(iii) *A incompletely specialized, B and C completely specialized.* As in our discussion of case (i), we proceed initially under the protective assumption that world prices remain constant in the face of the exchange of preferences. The immediate effect of the exchange is to render investment in A more profitable for residents of B. Capital therefore flows from B to A, thus raising its marginal productivity in B. The flow continues until, net of tax, the two marginal returns are brought into equality. In the new equilibrium the marginal productivity of capital is lower in B, unchanged in A and C. A is a greater debtor, B a greater creditor, than in the initial equilibrium and C's debtor-creditor position is unchanged.

Evidently C is left neither better off nor worse off. And B clearly is better off as the result of the tax concession extended by A. A on the other hand may be either better off or worse off. Evidently A suffers from the loss of taxes levied on the initial B-earnings. The initial taxes are, in terms of the first commodity,

$$-t^A K^B M_1^A p_1^A / p_1 = -t^A K^B M_1^A (1 + \tau_1^A)$$

and the loss of taxes on the initial B-earnings is

$$dt^A K^B M_1^A (1 + \tau_1^A). \tag{3.12}$$

However this loss may be more than offset by the inflow of new B-capital. The increase in A's output is $-M_1^A dK^B$. From this A pays to B, after tax, $-(1 - t^A - dt^A)M_1^A(1 - \tau_1^A)dK^B$, leaving a balance of $-M_1^A[1 - (1 - t^A - dt^A)(1 + \tau_1^A)]dK^B$ which may be positive and, indeed, may exceed the expression (3.12).

Thus if world prices are undisturbed by the exchange of preferences we may be sure that C's welfare is unaffected and that B benefits; A's welfare may improve or deteriorate. But of course prices do change. In B, output of the first commodity declines and, inferiority aside, demand increases; B's net demand therefore expands. C's net demand does not change, and A's increases or decreases according as the first industry in A is relatively labour-intensive or relatively capital-intensive. Thus the world price ratio may move in either direction but must move in favour of the first commodity if in A the first industry is relatively labour-intensive. As in earlier cases, we must examine those further effects of tax preferences which come into play as the result of changes in commodity prices. Here attention is confined to the subcase in which A's second industry is relatively capital-intensive, leaving to the reader the examination of the alternative possibility. For concreteness, it is supposed that the relative price of the second commodity increases.

For B and C the price change is unambiguously beneficial. The terms of trade deteriorate but this is more than offset by the improvement in the return to foreign investment. Consider the outcome for C. The increase in C's foreign receipts is, in terms of the first commodity,

$$-(1 - t^A)(1 + \tau_1^A)K^C M_1^A[(dM_1^A/M_1^A) + (dK^C/K^C)]$$

and the increase in C's output is

$$M_1^C dK^C = M_1^A(1 + \tau_1^A)(1 - t^A)dK^C.$$

The net increase in C's disposable real income is therefore

$$-(1 - t^A)(1 + \tau_1^A)K^C M_1^A(dM_1^A/M_1^A)$$

which is negative. A similar expression may be obtained for B. For A, on the other hand, the price increase may be either harmful or beneficial. The real reward to foreign capital increases and, if the volume of trade is sufficiently small, this may outweigh the improvement in the terms of trade.[22])

NOTES

[1]) See section 1.1.

[2]) If country A imports neither commodity it will of course tax its exports of the first commodity. Then $\tau_1{}^A$ must be interpreted as the rate of export duty,

but computed on the foreign price as base. Computed on the domestic price the rate of export duty is $- \tau_1{}^A/(1 + \tau_1{}^A)$. Cf. our second convention (section 1.1).
[3]) Written in full, the condition is

$$M_1^A p_1^A (1 - t^A) = M_1^C p_1^C = M_1^C p_1.$$

Eq. (3.1b) is obtained by substituting

$$p_1^A = p_1^C (1 + \tau_1^A).$$

If it is a net creditor, A will tax the foreign earnings of its own residents. Then t^A must be interpreted as minus the rate of tax on foreign earnings, but computed on after-tax income as base. Computed on income before tax, the rate of tax is $- t^A/(1 - t^A)$.
[4]) For an analysis of nondiscriminatory tariff concessions in a world with capital mobility, see Kemp [5], ch. 10.
[5]) The after-tax earnings of foreign capital, in money terms, are

$$K^A M_2^A p_2^A (1 - t^A).$$

Converting at the world price p_2, and recalling that $p_2 = p_2{}^A$, we obtain the expression in the text.
[6]) If B borrows directly from C we have, as a condition of equilibrium in the international capital market, $p_1 M_1^C = p_1^B M_1^B (1 - t^B)$, whence $M_1^C = M_1^B (1 - t^B)$. The total amount paid in service of B's debt is, therefore, $K^B M_1^C = K^B M_1^B (1 - t^B)$. If B neither borrows from nor lends to C, we arrive at the same expression indirectly by making use of the fact that B borrows from or lends to A which, in turn, lends to or borrows from C. For example, if A lends to both B and C we have, in capital-market equilibrium,

$$p_1^B M_1^B (1 - t^B) = p_2^A M_2^A (1 - t^A) = p_1 M_1^C$$

whence $M_1^C = M_1^B (1 - t^B)$ again.
[7]) See note 6.
[8]) See note 6.
[9]) Alternatively, one could simply add all commodity imports and exports, valuing them at the constant world prices, and speak of trade creation if the total increases, trade diversion if the total decreases. Or one could avoid all ambiguity by including in the calculation trade in the services of capital.
[10]) See note 5.
[11]) See note 6.
[12]) After the formation of the investing club, B's foreign earnings are, in money terms,

$$p_2^A M_2^A (1 - t^A - dt^A) = p_2^A M_2^A (1 - t^A)[1 - dt^A/(1 - t^A)].$$

In capital-market equilibrium, however,

$$p_2^A M_2^A (1 - t^A) = p_1 M_1^C.$$

[13] For a more detailed statement of this part of the argument, see Inada and Kemp [3], and Kemp [5], ch. 10.

[14] The generalization of this result is of some interest. Suppose that m countries trade in n goods and that there are $q < n$ mobile factors. The possibility of incomplete specialization in all countries can be ruled out if $q(m - 1) > n - 1$.

[15] In money terms, C's initial foreign earnings are $-K^C p_2{}^A M_2{}^A (1 - t^A)$. Its new earnings are $-(K^C + dK^C) p_2{}^A (M_2{}^A + dM_2{}^A)(1 - t^A)$. The increase in its earnings is, therefore,

$$-p_2^A K^C M_2^A (1 - t^A)[(dM_2^A/M_2^A) + (dK^C/K^C)].$$

On the other hand, C's output increases by $M_1{}^C dK^C$ which, making use of the conditions of capital market equilibrium, can be expressed as $p(1 - t^A)M_2{}^A dK^C$. Expressing the increase in earnings in terms of the first commodity and adding to the increase in output, we obtain the increase in C's real disposable income.

[16] In terms of the second commodity, A's initial debt service is

$$-K^B M_2{}^A (1 - t^A - dt^A) - K^C M_2{}^A (1 - t^A)$$

where the first term represents payments to B and the second represents payments to C, and where K^B, K^C and $M_2{}^A$ are assumed to have adjusted to the exchange of tax preferences (but, of course, not to the change in commodity prices). A's new debt service is

$$-(K^B + dK^B)(M_2^A + dM_2^A)(1 - t^A - dt^A) - $$
$$- (K^C + dK^C)(M_2^A + dM_2^A)(1 - t^A)$$

and the increase

$$-K^B M_2^A[(dM_2^A/M_2^A) + (dK^B/K^B)](1 - t^A - dt^A) - $$
$$- K^C M_2^A[(dM_2^A/M_2^A) + (dK^C/K^C)](1 - t^A).$$

The increase in A's output, on the other hand, is

$$M_2^A dK^A = -M_2^A(dK^B + dK^C).$$

The net increase in A's real disposable income, in terms of the second commodity is, therefore,

$$K^A M_2^A \left[t^A \frac{dK^A}{K^A} - (1 - t^A) \frac{dM_2^A}{M_2^A} \right]$$

which is positive.

[17]) The increase in the amount of the first commodity which, before trade but after the receipt of foreign earnings, C has at its disposal is, say,

$$dx_1^C = (\partial y_1^C/\partial p)dp + (\partial y_1^C/\partial K^C)dK^C$$

where y_i^C is the output of the ith commodity in C. Similarly, the increase in the amount of the second commodity which, before trade, C has at its disposal is

$$dx_2^C = (\partial y_2^C/\partial p)dp + (\partial y_2^C)\partial K^C)dK^C -$$
$$- K^C M_2^A(1 - t^A)\left(\frac{dM_2^A}{M_2^A} + \frac{dK^C}{K^C}\right)$$

where the third term on the right represents the increase in C's foreign receipts (see note 16). The combined value of the two increments, in terms of the first commodity, is $dx_1^C + (p + dp)dx_2^C$. Making use of the facts (a) that $(\partial y_1^C/\partial p) + p(\partial y_2^C/\partial p) = 0$, (b) that $(\partial y_1^C/\partial K^C) + p(\partial y_2^C/\partial K^C) = M_1^C$, and (c) that in capital-market equilibrium $M_1^C = pM_2^A(1 - t^A)$, the value of the two increments is simply

$$- pK^C(1 - t^A)dM_2^A$$

which is negative. In addition, the terms of trade move against C; *a fortiori*, therefore, C suffers from the change in world prices. Fig. 3.5 illustrates the argument.

[18]) The increase in B's foreign earnings, in terms of the second commodity, is

$$- K^B M_2^A(1 - t^A - dt^A)\left(\frac{dM^A}{M_2^A} + \frac{dK^B}{K^B}\right).$$

B's initial output, in terms of the second commodity, is y_1^B/p; B's new output is $(y_1^B + M_1^B\ dK^B)/(p + dp)$, that is, $(y_1^B + M_1^B dK^B)[1 - (dp/p)]/p$. The increase in B's output is, therefore, $[M_1^B dK^B - y_1^B(dp/p)]/p$. Substituting for M_1^B from the condition of capital-market equilibrium, $M_1^B = pM_2^A(1 - t^A - dt^A)/(1 - t^B - dt^B)$, and adding to the increase in foreign earnings, we obtain the net increase in B's disposable real income, in terms of the second commodity:

$$K^B M_2^A(1 - t^A - dt^A)\left(\frac{t^B + dt^B}{1 - t^B - dt^B} \cdot \frac{dK^B}{K^B} - \frac{dM^A}{M_2^A}\right) - \frac{y_1^B}{p} \cdot \frac{dp}{p}.$$

Since $K^B < 0$, $dK^B > 0$, $t^B + dt^B < 0$ and $dM_2^A < 0$, the expression is negative.

[19]) From the expression given in note 16 it is clear that real disposable income, in terms of the second commodity, must fall. This suffices to establish the possibility that A may be worse off. By a line of reasoning similar to that displayed in note 16, it can be shown that real disposable income in terms

of the first commodity may change in either direction, which establishes the possibility that A may benefit from the price change.

[20]) The directly price-induced increase in C's output, in terms of the second commodity, is $(1/p)[dy_1^C + pdy_2^C - (dp/p)y_1^C] = -(1/p)(dp/p)y_1^C$. The indirectly price-induced increase in C's output, that is, that part of the increase traceable to the price-induced inflow of capital, is $M_2^C dK^C$. The net increase in C's output, therefore, is $-(1/p)(dp/p)y_1^C + M_2^C dK^C$. On the other hand, C's foreign earnings increase by $(1 - t^A - dt^A)dM_2^A$. The net change in C's real disposable income, in terms of the second commodity, is therefore

$$(1 - t^A - dt^A)M_2^A - (1/p)(dp/p)y_1^C + M_1^C dK^C$$

which may be of either sign.

[21]) This follows from the expression for the increase in B's real income, given in note 18. With $dK^B < 0$ and $dM_2^A > 0$ the expression may be of either sign.

[22]) It suffices to consider the case in which initially A imports something of the first commodity, so that τ_1^A must be interpreted as the rate of import duty. The increase in the amount of the first commodity which, before trade but after the service of foreign capital, A has at its disposal is, say,

$$dx_1^A = (\partial y_1^A/\partial p)dp + (\partial y_1^A/\partial K^A)dK^A.$$

Similarly, the increase in the amount of the second commodity which, before trade but after the service of foreign capital, A has at its disposal is

$$dx_2^A = (\partial y_2^A/\partial p)dp + (\partial y_2^A/\partial K^A)dK^A$$
$$+ K^B M_2^A(1 - t^A - dt^A)[(dM_2^A/M_2^A) + (dK^B/K^B)]$$
$$+ K^C M_2^A(1 - t^A)[(dM_2^A/M_2^A) + (dK^C/K^C)]$$

where the third and fourth terms on the right represent the changes in payments to B and C, respectively, in terms of the second commodity. The sum of the two increments, valued in terms of the second commodity, is $[dx_1^A/(p + dp)] + dx_2^A$. Making use of the facts (a) that $p = p^A(1 + \tau_1^A)$, (b) that $(\partial y_1^A/\partial p^A) + p^A(\partial y_2^A/\partial p^A) = 0$, (c) that $[(\partial y_1^A/\partial K^A)/p^A] + \partial y_2^A/\partial K^A = M_2^A$, and (d) that $dK^A + dK^B + dK^C = 0$, the value of the two increments may be seen to be

$$\frac{\tau_1^A}{1 + \tau_1^A} \cdot \frac{\partial y_2^A}{\partial p^A} \cdot dp^A$$

$$-K^C\left[\frac{1}{1 + \tau_1^A}M_2^A + \frac{\tau_1^A}{1 + \tau_1^A} \cdot \frac{\partial y_2^A}{\partial K^A} - M_2^A(1 - t^A)\left(\frac{dM_2^A}{M_2^A} + \frac{dK^C}{K^C}\right)\right]$$

$+$ a similar term for country B.

The second and third terms may be of either sign.

CHAPTER 4

Free trade associations I

Throughout chs. 2 and 3 our attention was confined to infinitesimal tariff changes. We now approach the much more forbidding task of assessing the implications of finite tariff changes. In the present chapter we consider free trade associations under the simplifying assumption that international borrowing and lending are impossible. That assumption is relaxed in ch. 5. Finally, in chs. 6 and 7, we turn our attention to customs unions.

As in ch. 2 we suppose that three countries, A, B and C, trade in two commodities. Initially A levies an import duty the proceeds of which are distributed in lump-sum fashion to its residents; the same is true of B. The initial equilibrium is disturbed when A and B form a free trade association. We seek the implications for the pattern of world trade, for the welfare of each member country, for the welfare of the associated countries collectively, and for the welfare of the rest of the trading world.

To ensure that the problem is an interesting one, we suppose that initially, before association, A exports the second commodity, B the first, and that collectively the two countries export the second commodity (cf. ch. 2).

4.1. Constant terms of trade

We assume for the time being that the formation by A and B of a free trade association has a negligible influence on world prices, that is, on C's terms of trade. The more general case will be considered in section 4.2.

The pre-association trading equilibrium is again represented by

fig. 2.2, reproduced as fig. 4.1. At the terms of trade indicated by
OT, A imports OG of the first commodity and pays for it with OG′
of the second commodity. B, on the other hand, imports OH′ of
the second commodity and exports OH of the first. Jointly, A and
B export G′H′ of the second commodity in return for GH of the

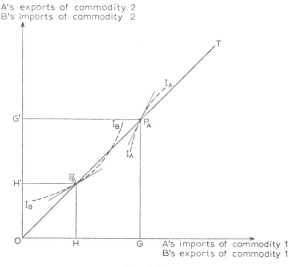

Fig. 4.1.

first. $P_A P_B$ is therefore the initial joint trading vector of A and B.

The initial trading equilibrium displayed in fig. 4.1 is disturbed
by the association of A and B. We seek now to depict the new
equilibrium.

Association makes possible duty-free trade between A and B at
the equilibrium, internal prices. Those prices depend on the direction
of their joint postassociation trade with the rest of the world. If
on balance they continue to import the first commodity the internal
price ratio must equal the world price ratio corrected by A's
import duty. If after association A and B jointly import the second
commodity the internal price ratio must equal the terms of trade

corrected by B's duty. Figs. 4.2a–4.2c illustrate three possible final equilibria. In each diagram P_A and P_B indicate the initial trading equilibria of A and B, respectively, and P'_A and P'_B indicate the final, post-association equilibria.

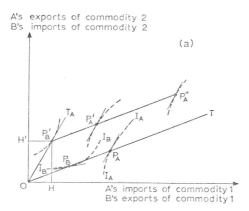

Fig. 4.2a.

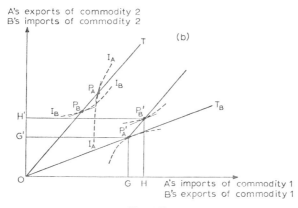

Fig. 4.2b.

Consider fig. 4.2a. In the new world trading equilibrium A continues to export the second commodity, B the first, and jointly they continue to export the second commodity. Since A continues to draw from C part of its supply of the first commodity, it is A's import duty which determines relative prices within the free trade area.[1]) At these prices, indicated by the slope of OT_A, B exports OH of the first commodity and imports OH′ of the second. All of B's trade is with A, hence P'_B is the appropriate origin for A's trade with the rest of the world. From P'_B A trades, at the given world terms of trade, to P'_A where the intersecting trade indifference

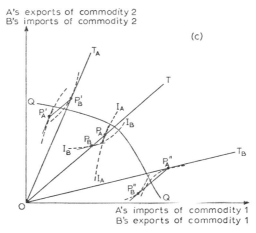

Fig. 4.2c.

curve has the appropriate slope. The joint trade of A and B with C is therefore indicated by the vector $P'_A P'_B$. The latter may exceed $P_A P_B$, in which case the association of A and B has *created* trade with the rest of the world; or it may fall short of $P_A P_B$, in which case the association has *diverted* trade.

It is easy to see that B must benefit from its association with A: its trade is freed of tariffs and its imports become cheaper.[2]) For A the outcome is less clear. Point P'_A illustrates the possibility that A will suffer from association; P''_A illustrates the opposite possibility. Notice, however, that for equilibrium to occur at P''_A it is necessary that in A the second or exported commodity be inferior in consumption. Moreover, inferiority strong enough to produce an equilibrium at P_A'' is also strong enough to produce multiple initial equilibria. Thus both P_A and P_A'' lie on the Engel curve defined by A's initial prices; between P_A and P_A'' this curve on the average is positively sloped; but there is an upper bound to A's exports, hence eventually, somewhere to the right of P_A, the curve must flatten out (and, possibly, assume a negative slope); it therefore must eventually intersect OT a second time, at say P_A'' (not shown). P_A''' represents a second possible initial equilibrium, superior both to P_A and P_A''. If instead of P_A we had chosen P_A''' as the initial equilibrium, we should have found that A is necessarily harmed by its association with B. In general the most preferred initial A-equilibrium is superior to any final A-equilibrium. If therefore we take care to choose the most preferred of the alternative initial A-equilibria we may be sure that association will depress A's welfare, enhance B's.

The case illustrated by fig. 4.2a is, however, not the only possible. That figure is drawn on the assumption that, individually and jointly, A and B import the same commodity before and after association. Fig. 4.2b, on the other hand, illustrates the possibility that their association may cause A and B jointly to switch from importing the first commodity to importing the second. After association A trades with B to P_A', at terms of trade determined by B's import duty[3]) and indicated by the slope of OT_B, exporting OG' of the second commodity in exchange for OG of the first. B then trades with the rest of the world from P_A' to P_B' at the given world terms of trade, exchanging GH of the first commodity for G'H' of the second. This is a startling conclusion.[4]) It is perhaps worth emphasizing therefore that *trade reversal* does not require inferiority; the outcome illustrated by fig. 4.2b is possible even if both commodities are normal in consumption.

Clearly A benefits from its association with B: its trade is freed of tariff obstructions and the terms of trade move in its favour.[5]) B may be left worse off (as in fig. 4.2b) or better off. The latter outcome, however, requires both sufficiently strong inferiority to produce multiple initial B-equilibria and the choice of an initial equilibrium other than the most preferred. If we take care to choose the most preferred of the alternative initial B-equilibria we may be sure that association will depress B's welfare, enhance A's.

Finally, we note an interesting intermediate case in which the formation of a free trade association *extinguishes* all external trade and allows the internal price ratio to settle at some determinate point in the closed interval defined by the initial A- and B-price ratios. That in figs. 4.2a and 4.2b the equilibrium points P'_A and P'_B might coincide is obvious. Of greater interest is the possibility, illustrated by fig. 4.2c, that at A's initial prices the joint import demand for the first commodity is negative while at B's initial prices the joint import demand for the second commodity is negative. Evidently no external trade can take place and the internal price ratio must settle somewhere between the extremes defined by the initial A- and B-prices.[6]) The new equilibrium will lie on the 'contract locus' QQ, between OT_A and OT_B, wherever the common tangent is a ray through the origin. The two members will trade along that ray from the origin to the point of equilibrium.

If the two initial indifference curves $I_A I_A$ and $I_B I_B$ intersect or touch, as in fig. 4.2c, at least one member, possibly both, will benefit from association; otherwise, at least one member, possibly both, will suffer.

Consideration of the above three cases suggests the following propositions. *The association of A and B may result in the creation, diversion, reversal or extinction of their joint trade with the rest of the world. If before association each member trades to its greatest advantage and if in the final equilibrium the association continues to trade with the rest of the world, one member must benefit, the other suffer; specifically, that member which after association trades only with its partner will benefit, the partner suffer. If before association each member trades to its greatest advantage and if in the final equilibrium trade with the rest of the world is extinguished, either at least one member suffers or at least one benefits, depending on the relative positions of the two initial indifference curves; specifically, if the initial indifference curves intersect or touch at least one member benefits (strictly, at least one member is not harmed), otherwise at least one member suffers.* Since its terms of trade are constant the rest of the world is indifferent to the association of A and B.

It is striking that for both members to benefit it is necessary that all trade with the rest of the world cease. One wonders then whether by means of lump-sum transfers between members it might always be possible *without extinguishing external trade* to ensure that both members benefit from their association. To this and related questions we now turn. Suppose for the time being that inferiority is absent.

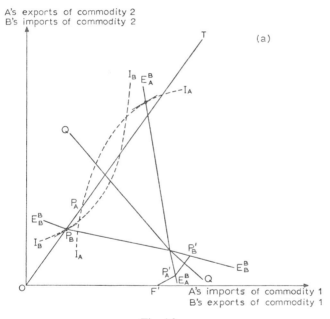

Fig. 4.3a.

We begin by showing that if neither member suffers from associ-ation trade reversal is impossible. The proof consists in assuming the contrary and then establishing a contradiction. First, however, we need some scaffolding. Consider fig. 4.3a. The initial A- and B-indifference curves again are labelled $I_A I_A$ and $I_B I_B$, respectively, and the initial A- and B-equilibria are indicated by P_A and P_B, respectively. The curve $E_j^i E_j^i$ is the Engel curve of the jth country defined by the initial prices of the ith country: of course, $E_A^A E_A^A$ passes through P_A and $E_B^B E_B^B$ passes through P_B. The contract locus is labelled QQ. Suppose, then, that in the final equilibrium A and B jointly import the second commodity and the internal price ratio settles at the initial B-level. A's final position must be represented by a point P_A' on $E_A^B E_A^B$, B's by a point P_B' on $E_B E_B$. Moreover, since A and B jointly import the second commodity, P_A' and P_B' must lie on a straight line parallel to OT, with P_A' south-west of P_B'. That line must lie either above both OT and a point of intersection of the Engel curves or below both OT and a point of intersection of the Engel curves. Finally, with inferiority ruled out, no Engel curve can have positive slope. It is easy to see that any pair of points which meets all of these requirements must at the same time imply a worsening of one country's welfare. Fig. 4.3a provides an illustration. A and B move from O to F' by compensation, with B paying to A an amount OF of the first commodity; they then move to P_A' by internal trade: and, finally, B trades with C from P_A' to P_B'. In the final equilibrium A is better off, B worse off, than before their association.

If after compensation neither member is worse off and if some foreign trade persists, then (i) the postcompensation A-equilibrium, indicated by P_A', must lie on $E_A^A E_A^A$ on or below the initial A-indifference curve, (ii) the post-compensation B-equilibrium indicated by P_B', must lie on $E_B^A E_B^A$ on or above $I_B I_B$, and (iii) P_A' and P_B' must lie at opposite ends of a foreign trade vector parallel to OT, with P_A' at the right-hand end and its associated point P_B' at the left-hand end. The three fold condition is also sufficient. In the assumed absence of inferiority, it in turn is satisfied if and only if $E_B^A E_B^A$ cuts $I_B I_B$ *on or below* OT *and there exists, between* OT *and the point of intersection, at least one point* P_B' *on* $E_B^A E_B^A$ *which lies to the left of its associated point* P_A'. If between OT and the point of intersection *each* point on $E_B^A E_B^A$ lies to the left of its associated point mutually beneficial association *implies* the preservation of some foreign trade; that is, trade extinction is impossible. Finally, we note that mutually beneficial, trade-preserving association necessarily involves trade diversion. The complete proofs of these propositions are left to the reader.

It is easy to see that mutually beneficial association is possible if the initial indifference curves $I_A I_A$ and $I_B I_B$ intersect or touch. However, the condition is not necessary. Moreover, for association to be mutually beneficial *and trade-preserving* it is neither necessary nor sufficient that the indifference curves have points in common.

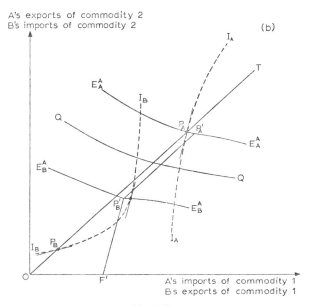

Fig. 4.3b.

That the condition is not necessary is illustrated by fig. 4.3b. The two members move from O to F′ by compensation, and from F′ to P'_B by internal trade; A then moves from P'_B to P'_A by trading with C. Although the initial indifference curves have no points in common, the italicized condition of the preceding paragraph is satisfied. That the present condition is not sufficient is illustrated by fig. 4.3c. Although the indifference curves intersect, the italicized condition is not satisfied. Mutually beneficial association is possible but implies the extinction of foreign trade. The final equilibrium will occur on the contract locus QQ, inside the 'ellipse' formed by I_AI_A and I_BI_B, with an internal price ratio somewhere between those prevailing initially in A and B. The members will move from O to F' by compensation, then from F' to P' by internal trade.

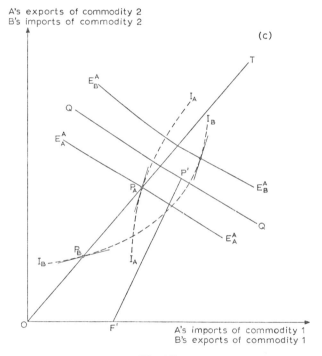

Fig. 4.3c.

If inferiority is admitted, some of these conclusions must be abandoned or qualified. In particular, the possibility of trade creation and of trade reversal must be recognized. Fig.4.3d illustrates the possibility that mutually beneficial trade-preserving association may create trade. Fig. 4.3d incorporates the assumption that the initial indifference curves have no points in common, but the same outcome is possible when the curves touch or intersect. Fig. 4.3e, on the other hand, illustrates the possibility that mutually beneficial trade-preserving association may reverse trade. It is easy to see that for trade reversal it is necessary that the initial indifference curves intersect. (In fig. 4.3e OG' is the amount of compensation paid by A to B, in terms of the second commodity; and the slope of $G'P'_A$ indicates the internal price ratio, equal in this case to B's initial price ratio.)

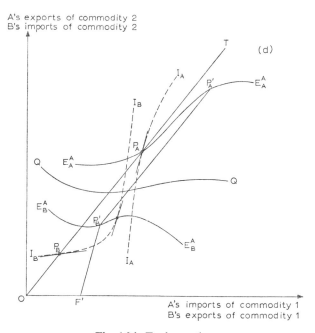

Fig. 4.3d. Trade creation.

However, while trade creation is sometimes possible, it is never inevitable. More precisely: if mutually beneficial trade-preserving association is possible with trade creation it is also possible with trade diversion. As fig. 4.3d makes clear, trade creation may be avoided by choosing a scheme of compensation such that the final equilibria lie sufficiently close to OT.

Trade reversal cannot be dismissed so easily. If for some schemes of compensation mutually beneficial trade-preserving association involves trade reversal, it always involves trade reversal. To help see this, note that mutually beneficial trade-preserving association can reverse trade only if the initial indifference curves intersect. Once that is understood, it is easy to see from fig. 4.3e that trade reversal can be avoided by choosing a scheme of compensation OG'' which guides the two members to a final equilibrium P''

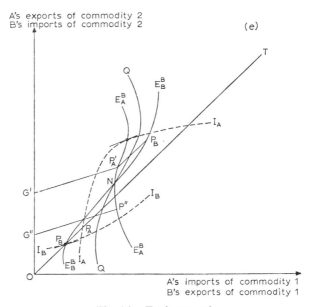

Fig. 4.3e. Trade reversal.

on the contract locus at or below N, the point of intersection of $E_A^B E_A^B$ and $E_B^B E_B^B$. At P'' external trade is eliminated and internal prices settle at a level between the initial A- and B-levels. It is also easy to see that it is impossible to eliminate trade reversal, while preserving the mutually beneficial character of association, without also eliminating external trade.

Our conclusions concerning the possibility of mutually beneficial association may be summarized in the following way. *Mutually beneficial trade-preserving association is possible if and only if* $E_B^A E_B^A$ *cuts* $I_B I_B$ *on or below* OT *and there exists, between* OT *and the point of intersection, at least one point* P_B' *on* $E_B^A E_B^A$ *which lies to the left of its associated point* P_A'. *In the absence of inferiority both trade creation and trade reversal are incompatible with mutually beneficial trade-preserving association. If inferiority is present, there may exist a scheme of compensation such that association is both mutually beneficial and trade reversing. If this is so, mutually beneficial trade-preserving association is necessarily trade-reversing; the only way to avoid trade reversal while preserving mutual benefit is to abandon foreign trade. For mutually beneficial association, possibly without trade preservation, it suffices that the initial trade indifference curves intersect or touch; this condition, however, is not necessary.*

These conclusions contrast with those reached in section 2.1. It was argued there that the formation of a small trading club is always desirable, in the sense that after compensation of the losers all members find themselves better off. We now find that, in the case of free trade associations, no conclusions of comparable sweep are available. *Sufficiently small mutual tariff concessions are always desirable, but the reciprocal abolition of duties is not necessarily so.* At this point we may recall a conjecture of Meade, Lipsey and Lancaster, that 'a partial preferential reduction of tariffs is more likely to raise welfare than is a complete preferential elimination of tariffs'.[7]) For the special case of two commodities and three countries examined here, the conjecture is both confirmed and considerably sharpened.

4.2. Variable terms of trade

The assumption that world prices are constant has helped us get our bearings. Now it must be relaxed and our earlier conclusions re-examined.

Let us return to fig. 4.2a, which illustrates the possibility of trade *creation*. If it is sensitive to changes in the joint import demand of A and B, the terms of trade must deteriorate. In the final equilibrium, moreover, A and B must continue to jointly import the first commodity. A deterioration of the terms of trade is therefore to the advantage of B and the disadvantage of A; our earlier conclusion – that A will suffer, B benefit, from their association – is simply reinforced.

In the case of trade *diversion* we do not get off so lightly. We concluded in section 4.1 that in this case also A must suffer, B benefit. Trade diversion, however, implies that if the terms of trade are sensitive to changes in demand they must improve; and

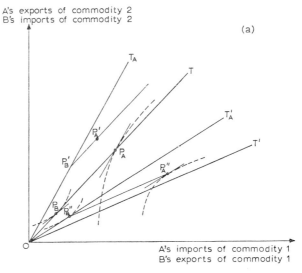

A's exports of commodity 2
B's imports of commodity 2

(a)

A's imports of commodity 1
B's exports of commodity 1

Fig. 4.4a.

this suggests the possibility that A may gain and/or B lose. Consider fig. 4.4a. The new terms of trade are indicated by OT' and the new internal price ratio by OT'_A. The new A-equilibrium is indicated by P''_A and the new B-equilibrium by P''_B. Clearly A benefits from association and B loses so that our earlier conclusions are turned upside down; in particular, the member harmed by association is now the member which in the final equilibrium trades only with its partner. Of course, such a radical revision of our earlier conclusions requires a very substantial improvement in the terms of trade. It is necessary that they improve so far that the new *internal* relative export price (indicated by the slope of OT'_A) is greater than the initial terms of trade (indicated by the slope of OT), that is, that the relative improvement in the terms of trade exceed A's rate of import duty; on the other hand, it is not necessary that the foreign import demand be inelastic. More modest changes in the terms of trade are associated with less sweeping changes in our earlier conclusions. It is possible, indeed, that those conclusions – that A suffers, B benefits from association – emerge

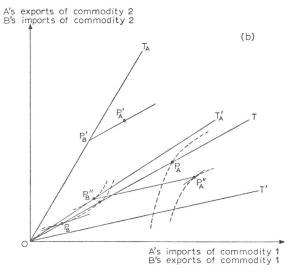

A's exports of commodity 2
B's imports of commodity 2

A's imports of commodity 1
B's exports of commodity 1

Fig. 4.4b.

unscathed. It is also possible for both countries to benefit (as fig. 4.4b shows). It is not possible, however, for both to suffer. To sum up: in the event of trade diversion at the initial terms of trade, at least one member will benefit from its association with the other; either member may benefit, either may suffer.

Trade *reversal* and trade *extinction* can be viewed as extreme forms of trade diversion. It is not surprising therefore that those welfare changes which we have found to be possible when trade is diverted are also possible when trade is reversed or annihilated. In the latter two cases, however, we must recognize an additional possibility: in the final equilibrium, after the terms of trade have adjusted, external trade may be nonexistent: and if the two initial indifference curves have no points in common both members may be harmed by association.

Thus our earlier conclusions concerning the effect of association on the welfare of members emerge almost intact after the relaxation of our assumptions about the world terms of trade; almost intact, but not quite. The revised conclusions are as follows. *The association of A and B may result in the creation, diversion, reversal or extinction of their joint trade with the rest of the world. If before association each member trades to its greatest advantage and if in the final equilibrium the association continues to trade with the rest of the world, at least one member must benefit; the member which benefits need not be the member which in the final equilibrium trades only with its partner. If before association each member trades to its greatest advantage and if in the final equilibrium trade with the rest of the world is extinguished, either at least one member suffers or at least one benefits, depending on the relative positions of the two initial indifference curves; specifically, if the initial indifference curves intersect or touch at least one member benefits (strictly, at least one member is not harmed), otherwise at least one member suffers.*

It is no longer true that the rest of the world is indifferent to the association of A and B.[8]) When its terms of trade change so does C's welfare. As we might expect, however, the relationship between the two is not quite straightforward. One suspects that C's welfare must increase if its terms of trade improve. This simple relationship does indeed prevail if C is a free-trading country; but if C is protectionist the relationship is more complicated. Consider fig. 4.5. At the initial terms of trade C is in equilibrium at P_C, where the intersecting indifference curve is tangential to an internal price line with gentler slope than OT. Suppose now that A and B form an association and that as a result trade is created. The terms of trade must move in favour of C. Suppose further that the new equilibrium occurs at P_C'. Evidently C is worse off than before the association of A and B. Notice, however, that the Engel curve $E_C E_C$ defined by the internal prices of the final equilibrium is on the average positively sloped between P_C' and P_C; that is, in C the first or export commodity is inferior in consumption. Since C's export capacity is limited, however, eventually, somewhere to the right

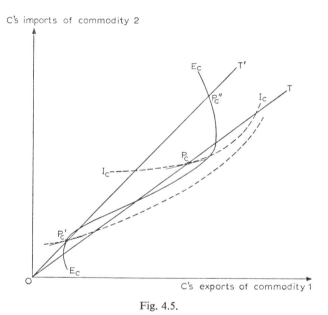

Fig. 4.5.

of P_C', the curve must become vertical (and, later, possibly of negative slope). It therefore must cut OT' a second time, at say P_C''. Point P_C'' represents an alternative final equilibrium. Moreover, it is superior not only to P_C' but also to P_C. If instead of P_C' point P_C'' had been chosen to represent the final equilibrium we should have concluded that an improvement in C's terms of trade results in an improvement in its welfare. In general, an improvement in C's terms of trade enhances C's welfare if in the final equilibrium C trades to its greatest advantage; similarly, a deterioration of C's

terms of trade depresses C's welfare if in the initial equilibrium C
trades to its greatest advantage.

We may conclude therefore that *if in both the initial and final
situations the rest of the world trades to its greatest advantage, the
association of A and B will benefit the rest of the world if and only if
association results in trade creation and will harm the rest of the
world if and only if association results in trade diversion (broadly
defined to embrace both trade extinction and trade reversal).*

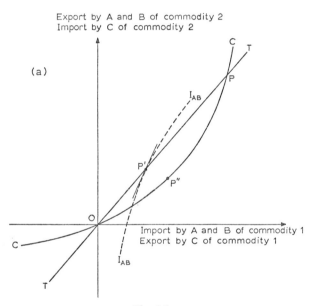

Fig. 4.6a.

It remains to consider whether with variable terms of trade
mutually beneficial association is possible. It will be shown that if
at constant terms of trade mutually beneficial association is possible
it also is possible with variable terms of trade. Suppose first that
mutually beneficial association is possible with trade diversion;[9])
and consider fig. 4.6a. The initial terms of trade are, as usual,
indicated by the slope of TOT; C's offer curve is labelled COC;

and the initial, pre-association equilibrium is indicated by point P. Now take any scheme of compensation which, had the terms of trade been constant, would have made the association of A and B mutually beneficial. To the postcompensation A- and B-equilibria which would have emerged there correspond two community indifference curves. From these curves we may construct a single joint indifference curve, say $I_{AB}I_{AB}$. In the hypothetical equilibrium with constant terms of trade, this curve is tangential to the internal price line, at say P' on TOT. Imagine next that $I_{AB}I_{AB}$ is imbedded in a family of indifference curves with the characteristic that as we move from one curve to another no two individual welfares (and therefore no two national welfares) move in opposite directions. From this family of curves, assuming that at each terms of trade A and B jointly trade to maximum advantage, we may distill the joint offer curve of A and B, distorted of course by A's tariff. This curve will pass through the origin and through P', and will cut COC to the left of P, say at P''. At P'' the terms of trade of A and B jointly have improved. Moreover, each member of the association is better off than at P' and therefore better off than at P.

If at constant terms of trade the postcompensation equilibrium involves trade extinction, a similar argument may be applied to demonstrate the existence of a scheme of compensation which ensures that association is mutually beneficial.

In the remaining case, in which at constant terms of trade mutually beneficial association is possible but involves trade reversal, the argument breaks down. However, the same conclusion can be established. Let us turn back to fig. 4.3e. It is easy to see that the curve $E_A^B E_A^B$ must cut $E_B^B E_B^B$ within the ellipse between P_B and P'_B, at say N on the contract locus. If A pays B an amount of compensation OG', in terms of the second commodity, and if the terms of trade are constant, N will be an equilibrium point with external trade extinguished and with both members better off than before association. If the external trade vector $P'_A P'_B$ had lain below OT, a similar argument would have revealed the existence of an equilibrium point below OT but with the same properties as N. Suppose now that compensation is such that at constant terms of trade equilibrium would occur at a point like N. Then we are back to the case briefly studied in the preceding paragraph.

We may conclude that if the initial indifference curves intersect or touch it is always possible to find a scheme of compensation which ensures that neither member suffers from association.

Suppose, alternatively, that the initial indifference curves have no points in common. We know from section 4.1 that in certain favourable circumstances mutually beneficial association is possible.

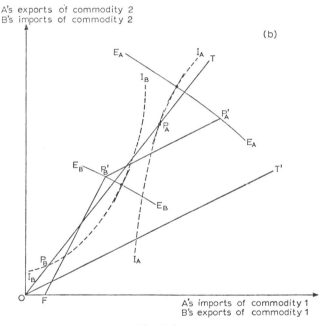

Fig. 4.6b.

We know also that, in these circumstances and in the absence of inferiority, the final postcompensation equilibrium will involve trade diversion. We have then a situation to which the long argument set out four paragraphs back can be applied without modification. If, however, inferiority is present mutually beneficial association at constant terms of trade may be associated with trade creation, implying that variable terms of trade will turn against the association. Does this mean that mutually beneficial association may be impossible? Consider again fig. 4.3d. Whatever the slopes of the Engel curves $E_B^A E_B^A$ and $E_A^A E_A^A$ it is always possible to find a scheme of compensation such that at constant terms of trade both members benefit from association and such that P_A' is sufficiently close to P_A to ensure that $P_A' P_B'$ is shorter than $P_A P_B$. In other words, even though for some schemes of compensation mutually beneficial association implies trade creation there always exist other schemes such that mutually beneficial association implies trade diversion.

Thus we may conclude that *if at constant terms of trade mutually beneficial association is possible it is also possible with variable terms of trade.* On the other hand it is possible that even when mutually beneficial association is impossible at constant terms of trade it yet may be possible if the terms of trade are variable; fig. 4.6b provides an illustration. Clearly much depends on the elasticity of foreign import demand.

NOTES

[1]) Before the association of A and B, the following price relationships are satisfied in equilibrium:

$$p_1 = p_1^A/(1 + \tau_1^A) = p_1^B$$
$$p_2 = p_2^A = p_2^B/(1 + \tau_2^B).$$

After their association, on the other hand,

$$p_1 = p_1^A/(1 + \tau_1^A) = p_1^B/(1 + \tau_1^A)$$

and

$$p_2 = p_2^A = p_2^B.$$

[2]) Given a country's terms of trade, the freeing of its trade results inevitably in an increase in its welfare; and given free trade, an improvement in a country's terms of trade can be relied upon to increase welfare. It is not true, however, that an improvement in a protectionist country's terms of trade inevitably

increases its welfare; at least, it is not true without careful qualification. These cryptic remarks are elaborated in section 2.2 and 4.2.

3) After association the following price relationships must be satisfied in market equilibrium:

$$p_1 = p_1^A = p_1^B$$
$$p_2 = p_2^A/(1 + \tau_2^B) = p_2^B/(1 + \tau_2^B).$$

4) It may be recalled, from standard, nonpreferential, two-goods tariff theory, that neither the imposition of a tariff nor its removal can reverse the direction of the tariff-imposing country's trade.

5) See note 2.

6) After the association of A and B the following price relationships must be satisfied in equilibrium:

$$p_1^A \geqslant p_1 \geqslant p_1^A/(1 + \tau_1^A) = p_1^B/(1 + \tau_1^A)$$
$$p_2^B \geqslant p_2 \geqslant p_2^A/(1 + \tau_2^B) = p_2^B/(1 + \tau_2^B).$$

7) Lipsey and Lancaster [6], p. 21. See also Meade [7], p. 51. The analysis of [6] and [7] is suggestive but it does not contain a proof of the proposition.

8) The reader may recall the discussion of C's welfare in section 2.2. The present paragraph summarizes parts of Bhagwati [1] and Kemp [4], which may be consulted for more detail.

9) Recall that if mutually beneficial association is possible with trade creation it is also possible with trade diversion. See above, p. 77.

CHAPTER 5

Free trade associations II

We seek now to extend our analysis of free trade associations by admitting the possibility of international factor movements. Throughout the present chapter it will be assumed that capital is perfectly mobile in the sense of ch. 3, that is, that capital distributes itself between countries in whatever manner will equalize returns after tax for the lending country. We confine our attention to the case in which A and B, individually and collectively, exert a negligible influence on world commodity prices and capital rentals.

As in ch. 3, and for the same reasons, it is assumed (i) that C trades freely and levies no income taxes, (ii) that both before and after their association A and B are completely specialized in production, A in the production of the second commodity, B in the production of the first, (iii) that initially A trades with both B and C whereas B and C trade with A only, (iv) that B both imports from and exports to A, and (v) that A imports a positive quantity from C.

Figs. 5.1a–c depict the three types of initial equilibrium which are consistent with the above assumptions. In each figure the trade indifference curves (and the production blocks which lie behind them) are defined by the stocks of capital initially installed in A and B. Consider fig. 5.1a, which illustrates the possibility that both A and B are in debt to C (so that, jointly, A and B both import from and export to C). The initial debt service of A, in terms of the second commodity, is $K^A M_1^A(1 - t^A)$; the initial debt service of B, in terms of the first commodity, is $K^B M_1^B(1 - t^B)$; and the joint exports of A and B, of goods other than capital services, are indicated by WP_A, the joint imports by WP_B. Figs. 5.1b and 5.1c, on the other hand, illustrate the possibility that C is in debt to both A and B. In fig. 5.1b A and B both import and export from C; in fig. 5.1c only one-way trade takes place.

The initial trading and investing equilibrium is disturbed by the association of A and B. We seek to describe the possible new equilibria. It will suffice perhaps to confine our attention to the initial equilibrium displayed in fig. 5.1a and to describe the three final patterns of trade and investment consistent with that starting point.

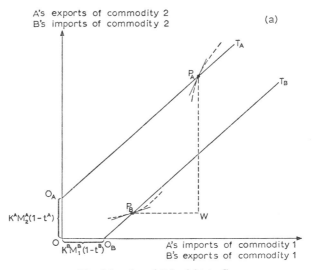

Fig. 5.1a. A and B in debt to C.

First we note the possibility that the final pattern of trade and investment may be similar to the initial pattern. Suppose, for the time being, that the net international indebtedness of A and B does not change as the result of their association; and consider fig. 5.2a. Since A continues to trade with C, A's prices are unchanged. Since on the other hand B's postassociation trade with A is unimpeded, B's terms of trade and internal prices must move in favour of the first or exported commodity. After association, B trades from O_B to P'_B along its new terms-of-trade line $O_B T'_B$.

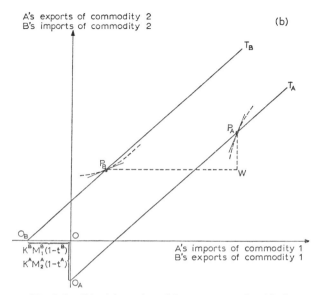

Fig. 5.1b. C in debt to A and B, two-way trade with C.

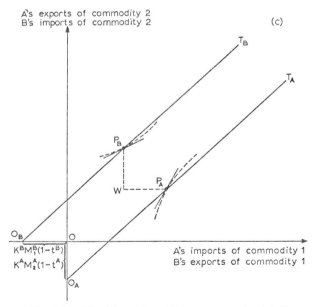

Fig. 5.1c. C in debt to A and B, one-way trade with C.

A then trades from O'_A to P'_A, where $P'_B O'_A = OO_A$ is A's constant debt service. Inferiority aside, A is worse off, B better off.

Dropping the assumption that the net indebtedness of A and B is constant we note that the increase in the price of B's output will result in an inflow of capital from C. This will depress the marginal physical product of capital in B until capital-market equilibrium is restored. In the new equilibrium B will be even more heavily in debt; but it also will be even better off, for it will reap an additional surplus on the capital inflow.

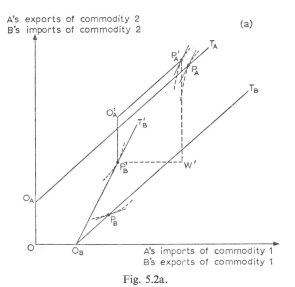

Fig. 5.2a.

In this particular case, then, inferiority aside, A will be harmed and B benefitted by association.

Next we illustrate the possibility that the association of A and B may result in the reversal of the direction of their trade with the rest of the world without changing the direction of net indebtedness. Fig. 5.2b is drawn on the assumption of unchanged indebtedness. It shows that, subject to that assumption, trade *reversal* is possible. Since in the new equilibrium B trades with C, B's prices must be unchanged; and, since A's postassociation trade with B is un-impeded, A's terms of trade and internal prices must move in favour of the second or exported commodity. After association, A trades from O_A to P_A' along its new terms-of-trade line $O_A T_A'$. B then trades from O_B' to P_B', where $P_A' O_B' = OO_B$ is B's constant debt service. Inferiority aside, A is better off, B worse off.

Dropping the assumption of constant net indebtedness, we note that the increase in the price of A's output will induce an inflow of

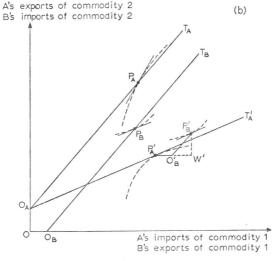

Fig. 5.2b.

capital from C. The inflow will continue until the marginal physical product of capital in A has sunk far enough to restore balance to the international capital market. In the new equilibrium A will be even more heavily in debt; but it also will be even better off.

In this second case, therefore, inferiority aside, A will benefit from association and B will be harmed.

So far our conclusions have run parallel to those of section 4.1. We now extend the parallelism by showing that association may result in trade *extinction*. Evidently trade extinction implies debt extinction too. That both trade and debt may be extinguished by association almost follows from the discussion of ch. 4. It is obvious that a postassociation equilibrium without external trade and without external borrowing or lending is possible; to see this one need only imagine that, in the final equilibrium on the contract locus of fig. 4.2c, there is everywhere no incentive for the owners of capital to lend abroad. It only remains to establish that such a final equilibrium is consistent with the initial equilibrium displayed in fig. 5.1a. We may satisfy ourselves that the two equilibria are

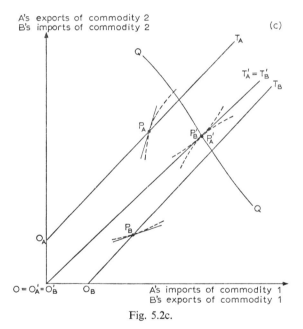

Fig. 5.2c.

indeed consistent by noting that as the result of association the internal relative price of the produced commodity falls in both A and B. It follows that the effect of association is to drive capital out of both countries. To establish the possibility of trade extinction one need only suppose that capital-market equilibrium is established precisely at the point at which all foreign capital has left A and B. The possibility is, of course, of little practical interest.

CHAPTER 6

Customs unions I

Again it is assumed that three countries A, B and C trade in two commodities, and that initially each country levies an import duty the proceeds of which are distributed in lump-sum fashion to its residents.

This time, the initial equilibrium is disturbed when A and B form a customs union, and we seek the implications for the pattern of world trade, for the welfare of each member country, for the welfare of the members collectively, and for the welfare of the rest of the trading world. Throughout the present chapter it is assumed that international borrowing and lending are impossible. That assumption is relaxed in ch. 7.

As in ch. 2, two cases are distinguished according as A and B are similar or dissimilar countries, that is, initially export the same or different commodities. The latter case, however, can be quickly disposed of. For if, as seems natural, we suppose that the union imposes on each commodity a duty equal to that imposed by the country which initially imported it, the customs union is indistinguishable in its effects from a free trade association and we may simply refer back to ch. 4. We shall therefore be concerned almost exclusively with the alternative possibility, that initially A and B export the same commodity, say the first. In a brief final section, however, an attempt will be made to summarize and relate to each other the principal conclusions of both chapters.

Some assumption must be made concerning the common tariff erected by the member countries. It is customary to assume that it is some sort of average of the initial rates of duty imposed by the member countries. In what follows therefore we shall for the most part confine our attention to two extreme alternatives: that the union adopts the higher or lower of the two initial duties. For definiteness it will be assumed that A imposes the higher initial duty.[1])

As a partial defense against boredom the treatment of inferiority will henceforth be confined to notes.

6.1. Constant terms of trade

Each country initially exports the first commodity so that, in terms of fig. 2.1, its initial equilibrium falls in the first quadrant.

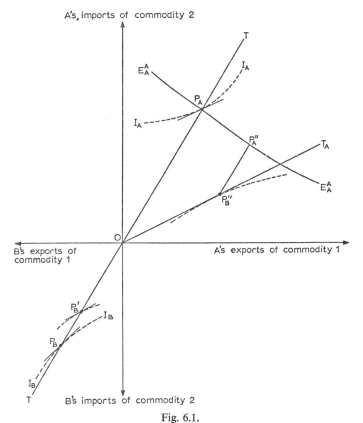

Fig. 6.1.

If B's diagram is rotated through 180° and superimposed on A's diagram, the result is fig. 6.1, in which the terms of trade are indicated by the slope of TOT and the joint trade vector of A and B by $P_A P_B$. The internal price ratios in A and B are indicated by the tangents to the indifference curves through P_A and P_B, respectively. In keeping with the assumption that A is the more heavily protectionist of the two members, the acute angle formed with TOT by the tangent at P_A is greater than the corresponding angle at P_B.

We begin by noting that *whichever initial duty is adopted by the union, trade reversal is impossible.* If trade were reversed, so that A and B jointly imported the first or duty-free commodity, the common tariff would be inoperative and internal prices would coincide with world prices. A would move to a new equilibrium on TOT further from the origin than P_A: similarly with B. However, such movements imply trade creation, not trade reversal. We may assume therefore that if they trade with C at all A and B jointly continue to export the first commodity.

6.1.1. Union with high level of protection

Suppose that the union adopts A's higher rate of duty. If after union A and B jointly continue to import the second commodity, the common internal price ratio will be that which initially prevailed in A. If, in addition, B continues to import the second commodity then, clearly, A's equilibrium and level of welfare are unaffected by union. In terms of fig. 6.1 the final, postunion equilibria of A and B are represented by P_A and P_B', respectively. B is worse off, A's position is unchanged; and union has resulted in trade diversion.

Faced with the possibility of trading at A-prices, however, B may choose to reverse the direction of its trade; that is, it may choose to export the second commodity and import the first, trading with A to P_B'' at terms of trade indicated by the slope of OT_A.[2]) Whether P_B'' is indeed a possible equilibrium point for B depends on the direction in which A seeks to trade (with C) from P_B''. If A seeks to trade in a north-easterly direction, that is, to import the second commodity, we can be sure that P_B'' represents a possible B-equilibrium; if A seeks to trade to the south-west it is seeking to do the impossible, as we have already seen, and we may conclude that P_B'' is not a possible B-equilibrium. The direction in which A seeks to trade from P_B'' depends in turn on the relation P_B'' bears to $E_A^A E_A^A$, the A-Engel curve defined by A's initial prices. (a) If $E_A^A E_A^A$ passes to the right of P_B'', as in fig. 6.1, A will trade in a north-easterly direction from P_B'', to say P_A'', and on balance the union will import the second commodity. Clearly A will suffer, while B may benefit[3]) or, as in fig. 6.1, suffer; thus at least one member, possibly both, will suffer. The vector $P_A'' P_B''$ is necessarily shorter than $P_A P_B$, that is, trade diversion is inevitable. (b) In the singular case in which $E_A^A E_A^A$ passes through P_B'', the latter lies on the contract locus and represents the equilibrium both of A and of B; trade with the rest of the world vanishes. A suffers while B may benefit[3]) or suffer; thus again at least one member, possibly both, will suffer. (c) If, finally, $E_A^A E_A^A$ passes to the left of P_B'', as it must when the initial indifference curves $I_A I_A$ and $I_B I_B$ intersect or touch, A will seek to trade in a south-westerly direction from P_B'', an impossibility. Trade with the rest of the world therefore vanishes, and the final equilibrium falls on the contract locus with an internal price ratio intermediate to the world and initial A-price ratios. If the initial indifference curves intersect or touch, at least one member will benefit from union (strictly, at most one member will suffer); if the curves have no points in common, at least one member will suffer.

Our conclusions to this point may be summarized as follows. *If the higher of the two initial tariffs is adopted by the union, trade will be diverted, possibly to the point at which external trade is extinguished. If the initial indifference curves intersect or touch external trade will be extinguished. If some external trade is preserved, at least the high-tariff member, and possibly both, will suffer.*[4]) *If external trade is extinguished and the initial indifference curves intersect or touch, at least one member will benefit (strictly, at most one member will suffer); if external trade is extinguished and the initial indifference curves have no points in common at least one member will suffer.* As with free trade associations, therefore, *mutual benefit implies the complete extinction of external trade.*[5])

Under what conditions can union supplemented by lump-sum transfers between A and B improve the welfare of both? Under what further conditions is this possible without extinguishing foreign trade?

The second question can be given an emphatic answer: mutually

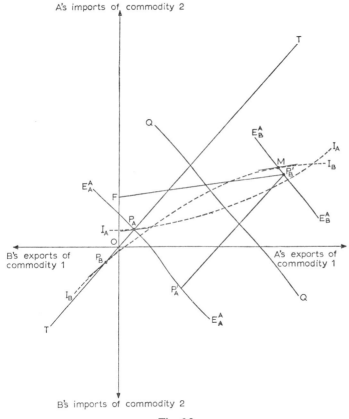

Fig. 6.2.

beneficial union implies the complete extinction of external trade. The proof is straightforward. We begin by showing that mutually beneficial union is incompatible with trade reversal. Suppose the contrary: that after compensation both A and B are better off and that jointly they import the first commodity. Then the internal prices of the union must coincide with world prices. For this reason and because A is better off, the final postcompensation A-equilibrium must lie north of P_A; for similar reasons, the final B-equilibrium must lie south of P_B. But this implies trade creation, a contradiction. Thus if in the postcompensation equilibrium A and B jointly continue to trade with the rest of the world that trade must be in the same direction as before union.

Consider now fig. 6.2. Mutually beneficial union, with external trade preserved, implies that the final A-equilibrium lies above P_A on $E_A^A E_A^A$ and that the final B-equilibrium lies on $E_B^A E_B^A$ below M, where M may lie in the first quadrant (as in fig. 6.2) or in the third or fourth quadrant. Consider *any* point P_B' on $E_B^A E_B^A$ below M. This point will be attained by B if B pays to A in compensation an amount OF in terms of the second commodity and then trades with A from F to P_B' at internal prices indicated by the slope of FP_B'. A then may trade with C from P_B' along a line parallel to TOT. Since that line lies below TOT, however, it must intersect $E_A^A E_A^A$ below P_A; that is, if in the final equilibrium some foreign trade is preserved it is impossible for both members to benefit. Thus mutually beneficial union implies the extinction of external trade. That a customs union between similar countries can improve the lot of its members only by annihilating external trade is something of a paradox.

It follows immediately from this proposition that if the initial indifference curves have no points in common mutually beneficial union is impossible. If they intersect or touch, however, it is always possible to find a scheme of compensation such that each member benefits from union (strictly, neither member is harmed by union). The appropriate compensation is found by first selecting a point which is both on the contract locus and within the critical 'ellipse' and then extending the common tangent associated with that point until it hits an axis.

In summary, *if the higher of the two initial duties is adopted by the union mutually beneficial union implies trade extinction, that is, the joint self-sufficiency of members.*[6]*) If the initial indifference curves have no points in common, mutually beneficial union is impossible; otherwise, it is possible.*[7]*)*

6.1.2. Union with low level of protection

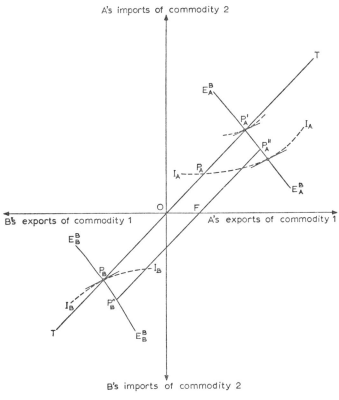

Fig. 6.3.

If B's lower rate of duty is adopted by the union, very different conclusions emerge. B's initial price ratio prevails within the union; hence B's equilibrium is undisturbed and A is encouraged by the lower price of imports to trade more extensively with C, to say

P'_A in fig. 6.3. Thus *union creates trade, benefits the initially high-tariff country and leaves unchanged the welfare of the low-tariff country.*[8])

In view of this conclusion it is not surprising that *in this case one can always find a scheme of compensation which ensures that union is mutually beneficial.* Imagine, for example, that A pays to B an amount OF of the first commodity. A then will trade to P''_A, which is preferred to P_A; and B will trade to P''_B which is preferred to P_B. *Trade creation is an inevitable accompaniment of mutually beneficial union.*[9])

6.1.3. Union with average level of protection

We have confined our attention to unions which adopt as their common rate of import duty the higher or the lower of the initial A- and B-rates. Between these extremes fall unions with common duties defined by some kind of average. We cannot consider all

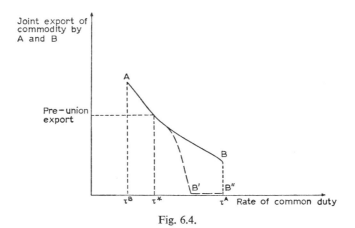

Fig. 6.4.

possibilities. However we may note, as an immediate implication of propositions already established, that *there always exists a common duty of intermediate magnitude which leaves unchanged the* *volume and direction of foreign trade.* In the illustration provided by fig. 6.4, τ_A and τ_B represent the initial rates of duty in A and B, respectively, and τ^* is the critical common rate which leaves foreign trade unchanged. The curves AB and AB'B″ describe alternative relationships between the common tariff and the volume of foreign trade. *If that critical rate of duty is adopted, the initially high-tariff country will benefit from union; possibly both members will benefit.*

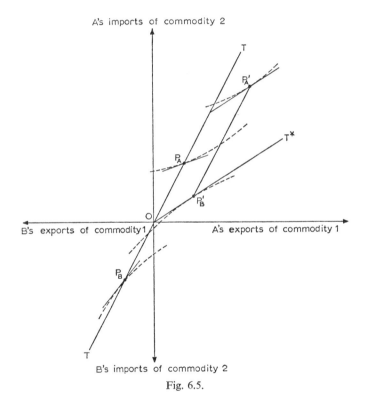

A's imports of commodity 2

B's exports of commodity1

A's exports of commodity 1

B's imports of commodity 2

Fig. 6.5.

This is obvious if the initially low tariff country B continues to import the first commodity. For then, in terms of figs. 6.1–6.3, P'_B must lie on TOT between O and P_B, implying that B is worse off; and P'_A must lie on TOT north-east of P_A, implying that A is better off. To see that the proposition is also true when the initially low-tariff country reverses the direction of its trade, suppose the contrary. In terms of fig. 6.5, B trades with A to P'_B at terms of trade OT^* intermediate to the initial A- and B-price ratios. A then trades with C to P'_A at the world terms of trade. By assumption, $P'_A P'_B$ is equal to $P_A P_B$ and the A-indifference curve which passes through P'_A cuts TOT south-west of P_A. On the other hand, the indifference curve must lie everywhere above or on its tangent at P'_A and, by construction, that tangent cuts TOT *north-east* of P_A. From this contradiction the proposition follows.

If the critical common duty τ^* is adopted, it may not be possible to find a scheme of compensation such that both members benefit from union. On the other hand we already know that *there exists a common intermediate duty under which mutually beneficial union is always possible,* viz. B's initial duty. It is not difficult to see that B's initial duty is merely the extreme member of a range of intermediate duties with that pleasant property.

6.2. Variable terms of trade

The assumption of given terms of trade has provided us with a special case of some theoretical interest. The main purpose of section 6.1, however, was to prepare the ground for an attack on the more general case in which the terms of trade are variable.

6.2.1. Union with high level of protection

In section 6.1 it was found that if the higher of the two initial duties is adopted by the union and if some external trade is preserved then at least one member, possibly both, must suffer. We also found, however, that union results in trade diversion. It follows that under our present more general assumptions the terms of trade must move in favour of the union. This in turn suggests the possibility that both members may benefit even though the union continues to trade with the rest of the world. That this may indeed be the outcome is illustrated by figs. 6.6a and 6.6b. Fig. 6.6a illustrates the possibility that in the final equilibrium, as in the initial equilibrium, both countries export the first commodity; fig. 6.6b illustrates the possibility that B, the initially low-tariff member,

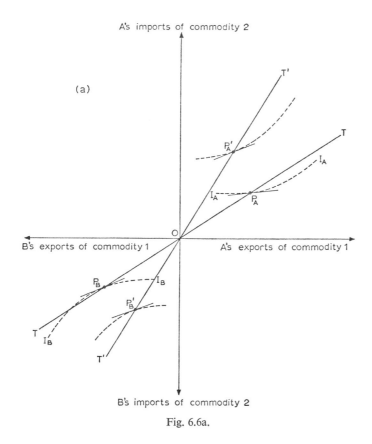

Fig. 6.6a.

switches from the export of the second commodity to the export of the first. In neither figure do the initial indifference curves $I_A I_A$ and $I_B I_B$ have points in common; the same possibilities may be realized, however, even when the curves intersect or touch. On the other hand, it is still possible that one or both members will suffer from union, in spite of the improvement in the terms of trade. (Fig. 6.6c illustrates the possibility that both members will suffer.) For the high-tariff member to suffer, however, it is necessary that the low-tariff member reverse the direction of its trade; and

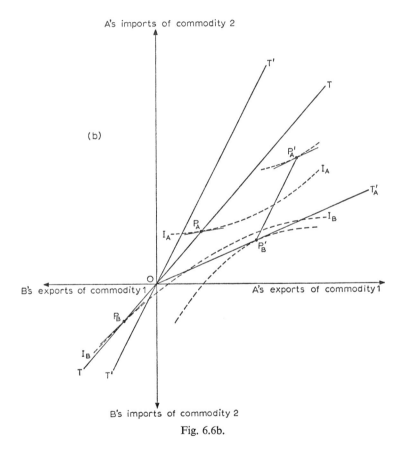

Fig. 6.6b.

for both members to suffer it is necessary that the initial indifference curves have no points in common.

We conclude therefore that *when the customs union adopts the higher of the two levels of protection anything can happen: both members may benefit, both may suffer, or one may benefit, the other suffer.*

The outcome for the rest of the world, on the other hand, is quite unambiguous. At constant terms of trade union diverts or

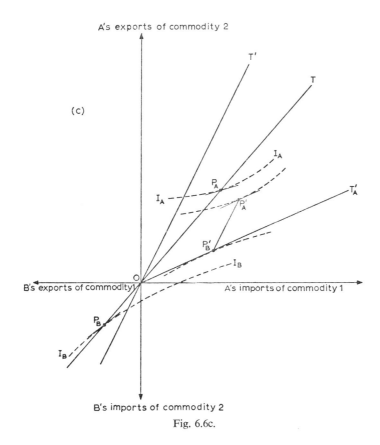

Fig. 6.6c.

extinguishes foreign trade. Hence the terms of trade must move against the rest of the world. We may conclude therefore that *union of similar countries with a high common rate of duty will harm the rest of the world.*

Under what conditions is it possible to find a scheme of com-

pensation which ensures that union is mutually beneficial? In
section 6.1 we learned to distinguish between situations in which
the initial trade indifference curves intersect or touch and situations
in which the curves have no points in common. The distinction

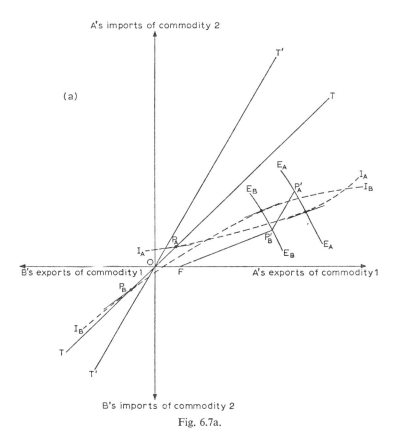

Fig. 6.7a.

remains useful. In the course of our earlier discussion we found
that if the curves intersect or touch, mutually beneficial union is
possible and that the postcompensation equilibrium must fall on
the contract locus within the critical ellipse, with all external trade
extinguished. Those conclusions were based on the assumption

that the terms of trade are constant. If in fact the terms of trade are variable they must move in favour of the union. *A fortiori*, mutually beneficial union is possible. It is possible, moreover, that in the final postcompensation equilibrium some trade with C is

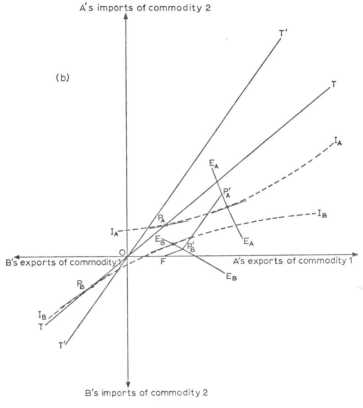

Fig. 6.7b.

preserved; fig. 6.7a provides an illustration. On the other hand, we found that if the two curves have no points in common mutually beneficial union is impossible. It also became clear, however, that trade diversion must be a feature of any final equilibrium. If follows that if in fact the terms of trade are variable they must change to the advantage of the union. This suggests the possibility that, after all, mutually beneficial union may be possible. That this may indeed be the outcome is illustrated by fig. 6.7b.

Thus *if mutually beneficial union is possible with constant terms of trade it is possible with variable terms of trade. When the terms of trade are constant mutually beneficial union is possible if and only if the initial indifference curves intersect or touch; when the terms of trade are variable this becomes merely an over-strong sufficient condition. Mutually beneficial union does not imply trade extinction if the terms of trade are variable.*

6.2.2. Union with low level of protection

We discovered in section 6.1 that, if the terms of trade are given, union with a low level of protection leaves the initially high-tariff member better off and the initially low-tariff member as well off as before union. We also found, however, that union creates trade. It follows that when the terms of trade are variable they must turn *against* the union, suggesting that after all one or both of the two members may suffer by joining the union. Indeed it may seem obvious that the initially low-tariff member must suffer and that the only question in need of attention concerns the welfare of the initially high-tariff country. In fact, however, literally anything can happen, even in the absence of inferiority: both members may benefit from union; both may suffer; or either may benefit, the other suffer. Fig. 6.8a illustrates the possibility that both members benefit; fig. 6.8b illustrates the possibility that both suffer; fig. 6.8c establishes the possibility that the initially high-tariff member benefits and the initially low-tariff member suffers; and fig. 6.8d illustrates the remaining possibility. Notice that for the initially low-tariff country to benefit it must switch from exporting the first commodity to exporting the second.

We found in section 6.1 that if the terms of trade are constant it is always possible to find a scheme of compensation which ensures that union benefits both members. This is so even when the initial indifference curves have no points in common. The final, post-compensation equilibrium is, however, characterized by trade creation so that, if the terms of trade are variable, they must deteriorate. If the initial indifference curves intersect or touch

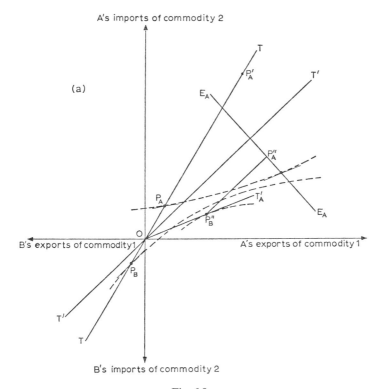

Fig. 6.8a.

mutually beneficial union is still possible. However, it is not difficult to show that if the indifference curves have no points in common then for sufficiently inelastic foreign demand mutually beneficial union may be impossible.

Thus *if the union adopts the lower of the two initial rates of duty anything may happen: both members may suffer, both may benefit*

*or one may benefit, the other suffer. For the initially low-tariff country
to benefit, however, it is necessary that it switch exports. If the terms
of trade are constant it is always possible to find a scheme of compensation which ensures that both members benefit from union; if*

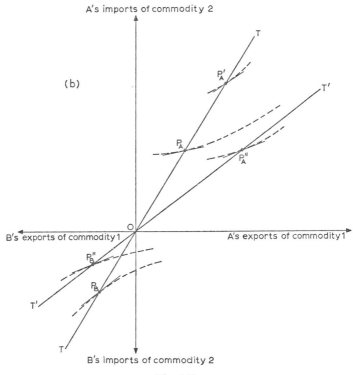

Fig. 6.8b.

*the terms of trade are variable, for mutually beneficial union it
suffices that the initial indifference curves intersect or touch.*

The outcome for the rest of the world, however, is unambiguous.
At constant terms of trade union is trade-creating; hence the terms
of trade must move in favour of the rest of the world. We may
conclude therefore that *union of similar countries with a low common
tariff will benefit the rest of the world.*

6.2.3. Union with average level of protection

We already know from section 6.1 that *there always exists a common intermediate rate of duty such that the direction and volume of the joint foreign trade of A and B is left undisturbed,* and that *if that rate of duty is adopted at least one member (the initially high tariff*

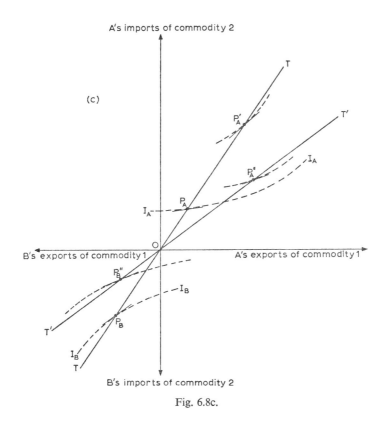

Fig. 6.8c.

member) will benefit. To that conclusion we may add, as an implication of conclusions reached in the present section, that *if there exists a common intermediate rate of duty such that with constant terms of trade mutually beneficial union is possible there also exists a common intermediate rate of duty such that with variable terms of trade mutually beneficial union is possible. For mutually beneficial union it suffices that the initial indifference curves intersect or touch.*

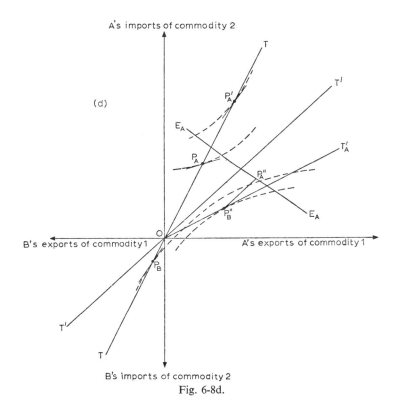

Fig. 6-8d.

6.3. Summary of conclusions concerning customs unions

In the present chapter we have traced the implications of unions of similar countries, unions of dissimilar countries having been treated implicitly in ch. 4. In this final section we summarize the principal conclusions of both chapters, confining our attention, however, to the most general case in which the terms of trade are variable.

The implications of union for patterns of world trade depend critically on the similarity or dissimilarity of the member countries and, if they are similar, on the level of the common tariff. If dissimilar countries unite, almost anything can happen: foreign trade may be reversed, extinguished, diverted, or created. If similar countries unite and adopt a high common tariff, trade will be diverted or extinguished; if similar countries adopt a low common tariff, trade will be created.

It follows that, if dissimilar countries unite, the rest of the world may benefit or suffer; that, if similar countries unite and adopt a high common tariff, the rest of the world will suffer; and that, if similar countries adopt a low common tariff, the rest of the world will benefit.

Simple generalizations concerning the welfares of member countries are much more elusive. Whether the members are similar or dissimilar and, if they are similar, whether they adopt a high or a low common tariff, anything can happen, the precise outcome depending on whether foreign trade persists and on whether the initial indifference curves intersect or touch.

NOTES

[1]) The case in which before union A and B levy the same rate of duty is trivial and may be ignored. Tariffs on trade between A and B will be eliminated; but before and after union such trade is zero. Union is therefore quite ineffective.
[2]) B will inevitably choose to reverse its trade pattern if the initial indifference curves $I_A I_A$ and $I_B I_B$ intersect.
[3]) If the initial indifference curves $I_A I_A$ and $I_B I_B$ intersect, B must benefit.
[4]) Vanek ([7], p. 50) incorrectly states that both countries must suffer if B's trade is reversed. He is wrong also, I think, in claiming that trade with C must decline if trade is reversed.
[5]) If inferiority is admitted, some of these conclusions must be qualified. Trade diversion is not inevitable. Nor, when some external trade is preserved, does the high-tariff member, or indeed either member, necessarily suffer. To challenge any of the conclusions of the text, however, it is necessary to introduce inferiority sufficiently strong to generate multiple initial equilibria. To preserve our conclusions it is necessary only to stipulate that in the initial equilibrium each country trades to its maximum advantage.

6) If inferiority is admitted, it is possible for both members to benefit without the destruction of external trade; indeed union may create trade. To preserve our conclusions in the face of inferiority, however, we need only add the familiar provision that initially each country trades to its greatest advantage.

7) If inferiority is admitted, this conclusion must be qualified in the usual way.

8) If inferiority is admitted, so must be the possibility that P_A' will lie southwest of P_A, implying that A is made worse off by union and, also, that union results in trade diversion. To preserve our conclusions it is necessary to stipulate that after union each member trades to its greatest advantage.

9) This is not true if inferiority is admitted.

CHAPTER 7

Customs unions II

We seek now to extend the analysis of customs unions by allowing for international factor movements. Throughout the present chapter it will be assumed that capital is perfectly mobile between countries so that marginal returns are for the lending country everywhere the same. As in ch. 5 attention is confined to the case in which, individually and collectively, A and B exert a negligible influence on world prices.

For reasons given in ch. 3 it will be assumed (a) that C trades freely and levies no income taxes, and (b) that both before and after union A and B are completely specialized in production. For reasons given in ch. 6 it will be assumed (c) that initially A and B produce the same commodity, say the first. It will be assumed also (d) that A and B import from C – otherwise, the preferential character of tariff concessions would be lost. As in ch. 5 we consider in detail only one case: that in which both A and B are in debt to C.

An initial equilibrium is displayed in fig. 7.1, which is a simple generalization of fig. 6.1. The initial debt service of A, in terms of the first commodity, is $K^A M_1^A (1 - t^A)$, represented by OO_A; and the initial debt service of B, also in terms of the first commodity, is $K^B M_1^B (1 - t^B)$, represented by OO_B. A trades with C from O_A to P_A; and B trades with C from O_B to P_B. As in ch. 6 it is assumed that A is the more heavily protectionist of the two union members.

The initial trading and investing equilibrium is disturbed by the union of A and B. We seek to describe the possible new equilibria.

We begin by noting that *whichever initial duty is adopted by the union, trade reversal is impossible*. The essentials of a proof may be found in section 6.1. Thus if trade were reversed so that A and B jointly imported the first or duty-free commodity, the common tariff would be inoperative and internal prices would coincide with world prices. In the absence of price-induced capital movements, A would move to a new equilibrium on $O_A T_A$ further from O_A than P_A; and similarly with country B. However such movements imply

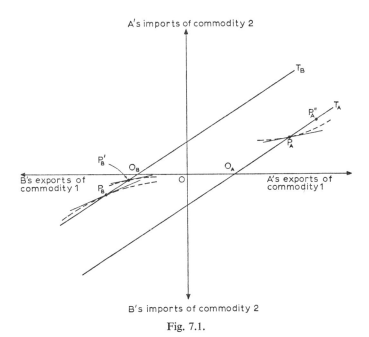

Fig. 7.1.

trade creation, not trade reversal. If they trade with C at all, therefore, A and B must jointly continue to export the first commodity. Allowance for capital movements merely reinforces the conclusion. For if trade were reversed the relative price of the initially-produced commodity (the first) would rise both in A and in B; hence capital would flow in (from C), A and B would sink deeper into debt, and in each country there would occur an increase in the output and (strong inferiority aside) in the export of the first commodity.

There is implicit in the preceding paragraph a rather strong definition of trade reversal: trade is reversed if both the imported and exported commodities reverse their roles. On an alternative weaker definition it might be required merely that the imported commodity reverses its role (so that, possibly, A and B after union jointly export both commodities). The above proof can be modified to establish the impossibility of trade reversal even in this weaker sense.

Trade reversal can be ruled out. Do our assumptions imply any further restrictions on the set of possible final equilibria? The question will be considered first under the assumption that the union adopts A's higher rate of duty, then under the assumption that B's lower rate of duty is adopted.

7.1. Union with a high level of protection

By constructing a sequence of simple examples it will be shown that, if a high level of protection is adopted, no further restrictions can be imposed on the set of possible final equilibria.

We first show that the final postunion equilibrium may display exactly the same pattern of trade and investment as the initial equilibrium, with A and B (and, therefore, A and B jointly) in debt to C and exporting the second commodity, importing the first. In such an equilibrium the common internal price ratio must stand at the initial A-level; in B the relative price of the second commodity must rise. Suppose that, in spite of the price change, B continues to specialize in the production of the first commodity,[1]) so that the return to investment in B (and therefore the level of B's indebtedness) must be unchanged. Then, with suitable B-preferences, a new postunion B-equilibrium may be found between O_B and P_B, say at P_B', in fig. 7.1; and A's equilibrium is, of course, unchanged at P_A. The points (P_A, P_B') represent the required equilibrium. A's welfare is unchanged, B is worse off; for each country the level of indebtedness is unchanged; and one can say without ambiguity that union results in trade diversion.

We next show by example that in the final equilibrium one member may be found to have reversed the direction of its trade without disturbing the initial pattern of trade and investment for A and B jointly. In an equilibrium with these features the common internal price ratio of A and B must stand at the initial A-level. Suppose that at postunion prices and the pre-union level of indebtedness B chooses to switch specialization and reverse the

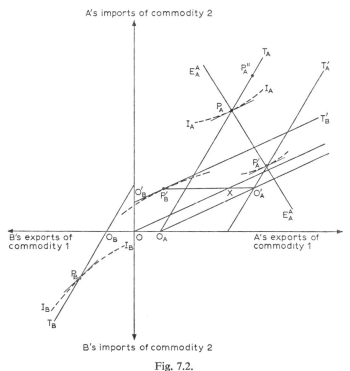

Fig. 7.2.

direction of its trade, importing the first commodity (from A) and exporting the second (to A) at terms of trade given by A's internal price ratio. The return to capital invested in B by C may change in either direction, or may not change at all. Taking the simplest case, suppose that the return to capital in B (and therefore the level of

B's indebtedness) does not change;[2]) and consider fig. 7.2. In terms of the second commodity, B's debt service is OO'_B, where O'_B lies *below* the vertical intercept of B's initial terms-of-trade line O_BT_B.[3]) Suppose that B chooses to trade with A from O'_B along the trading line $O'_BT'_B$, the slope of which is defined by A's internal prices, to P'_B. Turning our attention to A, we note that P'_B indicates the total trade of A with B and that this trade is unbalanced, with B running a surplus sufficient to cover its indebtedness to C. To balance its own payments, therefore, A must achieve a trade surplus with C sufficient both to service its own indebtedness to C and to offset its intra-union deficit with B. Accordingly we measure off, to the right of P'_B, an interval $P'_BO'_A$ composed of two subintervals. The first of these is P'_BX, equal to B's debt service in terms of the *first* commodity, the conversion being made at the union's internal prices. The second subinterval, $XO'_A = OO_A$, is equal to A's own debt service. Having serviced the joint debt of the two member countries, A may be imagined to trade with C from O'_A, at terms of trade indicated by the slope of $O'_AT'_A$. Our construction is completed by imagining that A trades in a north-easterly direction, to P'_A.[4]) Evidently the new postunion trading opportunities available to A are inferior to the pre-union opportunities; A is therefore worse off as the result of the union. B may be better off or, as in fig. 7.2, worse off. Thus at least one member, possibly both, must suffer.

It is now an easy matter to construct an equilibrium with joint imports annihilated and exports limited to whatever amount is necessary to service debt. To obtain such an equilibrium it need only be supposed that, presented with the opportunity to trade along $O'_AT'_A$, A chooses to stay at O'_A.[5]) Again A benefits while B may benefit or suffer; thus again at least one member, possibly both, must suffer.

Still we have not exhausted all possibilities. Suppose that B's indebtedness is held constant at the initial level and that, confronted with the opportunity of trading with A at the initial A-price ratio, B chooses to trade to P'_B (fig. 7.2). Suppose further that A attempts the impossible by seeking to trade in a south-westerly direction from P_B'. Evidently the internal price of the second commodity must fall and in any new equilibrium must lie between the initial A- and B-levels. Only in a singular case, however, would such an equilibrium be a full equilibrium of capital and commodity markets, for it has been attained by holding B's indebtedness constant at its initial level. Suppose that in the quasi-equilibrium just defined the return to investment in B is below the initial level. Capital will return to C, thus raising its marginal productivity in B and, by curtailing the B-supply of the second commodity, forcing its price back towards the initial A-level. The outflow of capital will continue until a full equilibrium, embracing both commodity and capital markets, has been achieved. Such an equilibrium may not be reached until B's debtor-creditor status, and possibly that of A and B jointly, has been reversed. It is possible, indeed, that in the new equilibrium A and B jointly import both commodities. *In that weak sense* trade reversal is possible.

7.2. Union with a low level of protection

If, at the other extreme, A and B adopt B's lower rate of import duty, the set of possible outcomes is severely restricted. For the immediate or impact effect of union is to lower the A-price of the second commodity, leaving prices in B unchanged. Thus neither A nor B is provided with an incentive to change its specialization. In both countries, moreover, the marginal productivity of capital is unchanged, hence C has no incentive to vary its investments. Hence a new equilibrium for B may be found by searching along $O_\mathrm{A} T_\mathrm{A}$ to the north-east of P_A for a point P_A'' at which the intersecting trade indifference curve has a slope proportional to the initial B-price ratio (see figs. 7.1 and 7.2). The points $(P_\mathrm{A}'', P_\mathrm{B})$ represent a final postunion equilibrium. Clearly A is better off, B neither better nor worse off; and one can say unambiguously that union results in trade creation. All low-tariff equilibria are of this type.

7.3. Union with average level of protection

Comparison of the low-tariff equilibrium just described with the analogous high-tariff equilibrium (the first construction of the first subsection) reveals the following generalization: if the union adopts an average of the initial duties of the two members, and if the initial pattern of world trade and indebtedness is preserved, the initially high-tariff member must benefit, the initially low-tariff member suffer.

The rich variety of possible high-tariff equilibria contrasts sharply with the utter lack of variety of possible low-tariff equilibria. Evidently the variety of possible equilibria increases with the height of the common tariff wall. The reader may find it interesting to search out the critical intermediate rate of duty at which one may exclude each of the several types of postunion equilibria described in the first subsection.

NOTES

[1]) The assumption is not restrictive, at least in the present context. For suppose that the increase in the price of the second commodity causes B to abandon complete specialization. The marginal physical productivity of capital in the first industry will increase or decrease as the first industry is less or more labour-intensive than the second. If the marginal productivity of capital rises, capital flows in until B is specialized in the production of the second or relatively capital-intensive commodity; if the marginal productivity of capital falls, capital flows out until B is specialized in the second or relatively labour-intensive commodity. In both cases, therefore, it is inevitable that in the final equilibrium B is specialized completely in producing the second commodity. We may conclude that, if in the final equilibrium B is specialized in producing the first commodity, it must be at all stages of the transition from the initial equilibrium.

[2]) This implies that $p_1 M_1^B(K^B) = p_2^B M_2^B(K^B) = p_2(1 + \tau_2^A) M_2^B(K^B)$, a restriction on production functions consistent with other assumptions.

[3]) The new debt service is $(1 - t^B) K^B M_2^B(K^B)$ or, from the preceding note, $(1 - t^B) K^B M_1^B(K^B)/p(1 + \tau_2^A)$, which is less than the vertical intercept $(1 - t^B) K^B M_1^B(K^B)/p$.

[4]) This choice implies that $E_A^A E_A^A$, the A-Engel curve defined by A's initial prices, passes north-east of O_A'.

[5]) This choice implies that $E_A^A E_A^A$ passes through O_A'.

CHAPTER 8

Optimal preferential trading arrangements

In chs. 2–7 we explored some of the welfare implications of free trade associations, customs unions, and other preferential trading arrangements. In particular, we set out the conditions under which both member countries could benefit by entering into such arrangements. At no stage, however, was it supposed that, jointly or separately, member countries were optimizing their trading relationships. The rate of duty on members' imports from the rest of the world, for example, was given quite arbitrarily and did not emerge as the solution to a maximum problem. Similarly, internal sales and production taxes and, in chs. 4–7, internal tariffs were equated to zero rather than their optimal values.

The purpose of the present chapter is to indicate how the deficiencies implied by the above remarks may be repaired. We begin in section 8.1 with unrestricted preferential trading arrangements, in which taxes and tariffs can be set at any level, and then in section 8.2 specialize by considering optimal trading arrangements when tariffs are subject to conventional upper bounds. Free trade associations and customs unions are treated separately in section 8.3. The possibility of international borrowing and lending is ignored throughout.

As a preliminary to any discussion of trade optima it is necessary to specify the criterion in the light of which alternative trading arrangements are to be ranked. Throughout the present chapter we shall continue to assume that in each country the distribution of income is discretely manipulated by ideal lump-sum transfers, so that the choices of each country are consistent with an Edgeworth-Scitovsky community utility function. An equilibrium is said to be jointly optimal for the member countries if for all feasible changes one member benefits only if the other suffers.

8.1. Optimal policy with unbounded tariffs

In the simplest imaginable case, the preferential trading community enjoys perfect freedom to set members' tariffs and internal taxes at any level, unconstrained by international conventions of any kind. Clearly it then will be optimal to clear away all internal taxes and tariffs and to confront the rest of the world with a common tariff schedule the elements of which are set at their familiar Edgeworth-Bickerdike optimal levels, leaving the intermember distribution of income to be adjusted by lump-sum payments. Although armed with additional fiscal devices, the community need not use them.[1]) In the joint optimum, therefore, the distinction between free trade areas, customs unions and other preferential trading arrangements can be made to disappear.

The optimal policy just described involves tariff discrimination: the community abandons all duties on internal trade while continuing to tax its trade with the rest of the world. It is of interest, then, that even when the community is bound by international convention to refrain from tariff discrimination it nevertheless may attain a full Paretian optimum. This is obvious if in the optimum the two members import the same commodity, for then all duties on internal trade are ineffective. Suppose, then, that only A trades with the rest of the world, importing the first commodity and exporting the second; and that B trades only with A, exporting the first commodity and importing the second. A is constrained to impose the same duty on its imports from B as on its imports from C. The internal price effects of that duty can be completely nullified, however, by the payment of a suitable subsidy on B's imports. (Of course, B is constrained to similarly subsidize its imports from C, but such imports are zero.) The distributional implications of the community's internal commercial policy can be corrected by lump-sum transfers between members.

Thus *whether or not tariff discrimination is outlawed, the community can reach a full Paretian optimum*. When tariffs are effectively bounded by international convention, a Paretian optimum is out of reach; but it remains true that the outlawing of discrimination is ineffective.

8.2. Optimal policy with bounds on tariffs

In this section we consider the fiscal-commercial policy problem faced by a preferential trading community when all tariffs are subject to conventional upper bounds.

Our problem is interesting only if the conventional bounds on tariffs are *effective*. In this connection it may be recalled that to any vector of external tariffs there corresponds a pair of consumption and production taxes which will achieve the same purpose. It follows that our problem is an interesting one only if the community is effectively constrained in its selection of consumption and production taxes. For the remainder of this chapter it will be assumed that the community is denied the use of production taxes so that, apart from the ubiquitous lump-sum taxes and subsidies, consumption taxes and tariffs on intermember trade are the only internal fiscal devices available to the community.[2])

If the conventional bounds are to be effective, they must at least preclude the imposition, on the joint trade of A and B with C, of the Edgeworth-Bickerdike optimal tariff vector. Granted that the bounds are effective in that minimal sense, there remain three cases for consideration. Thus it is possible that in the conventionally constrained optimum (i) only the duties imposed on the external trade of A and B lie at their bounds, (ii) only the duties imposed on the internal trade of A and B lie at their bounds, (iii) both classes of duty lie at their bounds. From a full-scale nonlinear programming formulation and solution of the problem one would learn, as part of the solution, which of the three possible outcomes is relevant. Here we simply deduce the properties of just one of the three types of optimum, type (i); that is, we simply *assume* that the conventional bounds on tariffs do not hamper the internal commercial policy-making of the community.

It will be assumed that the community may practice tariff discrimination. Later, however, it will be shown that to outlaw discrimination would not at all hamper the community.

8.2.1. A community of dissimilar countries

Suppose that in the optimum both A and the preferential trading community as a whole import the first commodity, with B trading only with A. The community's problem, then, is to find those taxes on consumption and those duties on intermember trade which make the welfare of the community as a whole a maximum. Among the constants of the problem are the tariffs on trade between the community and the rest of the world.

We have noted in section 8.1 that when the duties on trade with the rest of the world are set at their Edgeworth-Bickerdike optimal levels it also is optimal to remove all internal commodity taxes and all barriers to trade between member countries. One might be tempted to infer that the same internal policy is optimal when tariff conventions make it impossible to set the external duties at their Edgeworth-Bickerdike levels: if one cannot equate the internal marginal rates of substitution and transformation to the external marginal rate of transformation through trade, then at least one should ensure that the internal rates are equated. That this temptation should be resisted follows from the general theory of conventionally constrained optima (sometimes called the 'theory of second best'). A specialized formal proof will be given shortly. Since the proof is not easy, however, we first set out a rough common-sense account of the argument. Since the external tariffs are subject to effective upper bounds, foreign trade cannot be sufficiently restricted by tariffs applied directly to that trade. Further restriction can be effected by imposing in A a consumption tax on the first or imported commodity. Suppose that a very small tax is imposed. It will of course open a gap between the marginal rate of substitution in consumption and the marginal rate of transformation in A, and between the marginal rates of substitution in the two member countries; and that is bad. Since the tax is small and since the cited gaps are initially closed, however, the welfare loss from this source must be small in relation to the gain resulting from trade restriction. Now imagine that the rate of tax is progressively increased. The offsetting losses grow, whereas there must be point beyond which further restriction of trade is harmful. Long before trade is restricted to the Edgeworth-Bickerdike level, a point will be reached at which the marginal gains from further restricting trade and the marginal losses from further violating the internal marginal conditions exactly balance. Having reached that point, however, it will then be desirable to narrow the gap between the two marginal rates of substitution by subsidizing A's imports from B. The end result of this complicated manoeuvre will be to breach the internal Paretian equalities, but the associated loss of efficiency may be more than compensated by the improved terms of external trade.

To obtain expressions for the optimal set of internal taxes and duties we resort to a more formal analysis. With the *j*th country we associate a concave Edgeworth-Scitovsky utility function

$$u_j = u^j(x_1^j, x_2^j) \qquad\qquad j = \text{A, B, C,}$$

where x_i^j is the amount of the *i*th good consumed ($i = 1, 2$), and a convex set of production possibilities the boundary of which is described by

$$f^j(y_1^j, y_2^j) = 0 \qquad\qquad j = \text{A, B, C,} \qquad\qquad (8.1)$$

where y_i^j is the output of the *i*th commodity. The following additional notation is employed:

s_i^j ($j = $ A, B, C; $i = 1, 2$)   one plus the rate of consumption tax imposed on commodity *i* by by country *j*,

$s_i^A p_i^A$ ($i = 1, 2$)   the money price paid by the *consumers* of commodity *i* in country A,

p_i^A $(i = 1, 2)$ the money price received by the *producers* of commodity i in country A.

(In earlier chapters p_i^A stood both for the producers' price and for the consumers' price; with the introduction of consumption taxes, however, the two prices are pried apart and two symbols required.) Subscripts attached to f^j and u^j indicate partial differentiation; for example, $f_1^j = \partial f^j / \partial y_1^j$.

Under the assumed conditions of perfect competition the following equalities hold:

$$u_1^A / s_1^A p_1^A = u_2^A / s_2^A p_2^A \tag{8.2}$$

$$(1 + \tau_1^{BA})(1 + \tau_1^{BA*}) u_1^B / s_1^B p_1^A = u_2^B / (1 + \tau_2^{AB})(1 + \tau_2^{AB*}) s_2^B \tag{8.3}$$

$$(1 + \tau_1^{CA})(1 + \tau_1^{CA*}) u_1^C / s_1^C p_1^A = u_2^C / (1 + \tau_2^{AC})(1 + \tau_2^{AC*}) s_2^C p_2^A \tag{8.4}$$

$$f_1^A / p_1^A = f_2^A / p_2^A \tag{8.5}$$

$$(1 + \tau_1^{BA})(1 + \tau_1^{BA*}) f_1^B / p_1^A = f_2^B / (1 + \tau_2^{AB})(1 + \tau_2^{AB*}) p_2^A \tag{8.6}$$

$$(1 + \tau_1^{CA})(1 + \tau_1^{CA*}) f_1^C / p_1^A = f_2^C / (1 + \tau_2^{AC})(1 + \tau_2^{AC*}) p_2^A \tag{8.7}$$

$$\sum_j y_i^j = \sum_j x_i^j \tag{8.8}$$

$$p_1^A (x_1^C - y_1^C) / (1 + \tau_1^{CA}) + (1 + \tau_2^{AC*}) p_2^A (x_2^C - y_2^C) = 0. \tag{8.9}$$

The first six of these equations are familiar marginal equalities. Eq. (8.8) expresses the requirement that world consumption of each commodity should equal world production. Eq. (8.9) imposes equilibrium on the balance of payments between C and the preferential trading community (and between C and A, since B trades only with A). The balance of current account payments between A and B, on the other hand, need not equal zero; that balance will be equal to whatever compensatory payments are needed to hold u^A or u^B at its assigned level.

So far we have accumulated twelve equations and, if the s_i^j, τ_i^{jk} and τ_i^{jk*} are treated as constant parameters, thirteen variables: the x_i^j and y_i^j, and p_2^A/p_1^A. To complete the system we equate u^A or u^B to a constant, thus setting the internal intermember distribution of income:

$$u^j(x_1^j, x_2^j) = \bar{u}^j \qquad\qquad j = \text{A or B.} \qquad (8.10)$$

We seek those values of the eight policy parameters s_i^A, s_i^B, τ_2^{AB}, τ_2^{AB}, τ_1^{BA} and τ_1^{BA} which will push the equilibrium values of the thirteen variables to whatever levels maximize u^A or u^B, whichever is not constrained by eq. (8.10). (C's taxes and tariffs, s_i^C, τ_2^{AC} and τ_2^{CA*}, are of course among the constants of the problem. The same is true of the product $(1 + \tau_1^{CA})(1 + \tau_2^{AC*})$, which lies at its conventional upper bound.)[4].) Notice, however, that in eqs. (8.2)–(8.10) the terms $(1 + \tau_2^{AB})$ and $(1 + \tau_2^{AB*})$ appear only in product form, and that the same is true of $(1 + \tau_1^{BA})$ and $(1 + \tau_1^{BA*})$. There are therefore just six 'free' policy parameters to play with.[5]) To remind the reader of this fact the paired terms will henceforth be enclosed in braces.

Suppose that the six free policy levers have been set at their optimal positions and that the thirteen variables have assumed their equilibrium values. Then any infinitesimal and feasible change in the quantities produced, consumed and traded by the three countries should leave unchanged the level of the floating utility indicator, u^A or u^B. By considering particular examples of such changes, and in each case drawing out the implications of utility stationarity for the six policy levers, we may hope to discover the optimal levels at which they should be set.

As a first example, let $j = $ B in eq. (8.10) and consider a small movement along B's production frontier away from the optimal point, with equal changes in A's consumption. Suppose that such a change is feasible, in the sense that the new values of the variables would be established competitively if the six policy levers were set at appropriate levels. Then it is well known that the proposed change will leave u^A undisturbed if and only if A's marginal rate of substitution in consumption is equal to the marginal rate of transformation along B's production frontier. This equality must therefore be satisfied in the optimum. From eqs. (8.2) and (8.6), however, the equality will be established competitively if and only if[6])

$$s_2^A/s_1^A = \{(1 + \tau_2^{AB})(1 + \tau_2^{AB^*})\}\{(1 + \tau_1^{BA})(1 + \tau_1^{BA^*})\}. \quad (8.11)$$

It remains to establish that the proposed change is indeed feasible. To this end, set the x_i^A and y_i^B at their new suboptimal values. Treating the six policy parameters as variables, our system of thirteen equations now contains $15(= 13 - 4 + 6)$ variables, so that on balance we have two degrees of freedom.[7]) Is there, among the many available solutions, one in which the original variables other than x_i^A and y_i^B assume their initial values? It is obvious that eqs. (8.4), (8.5), (8.7) and (8.9) are satisfied by the initial values. By construction, eq. (8) is satisfied too. On the other hand eq. (8.3) is satisfied by the initial values only is $s_2^B\{(1 + \tau_1^{BA})(1 + \tau_1^{BA^*})\}$ and $s_1^B/\{(1 + \tau_2^{AB})(1 + \tau_2^{AB^*})\}$ bear their old relation to each other; and eqs. (8.2) and (8.6) are satisfied if eq. (8.11) is satisfied. The two degrees of freedom may be used to maintain the required relationships between the policy levers; hence the proposed change is feasible.

As a second example, let $j = A$ in eq. (8.10) and consider a small movement along B's production frontier matched by changes in B's consumption, with all other variables unchanged. That such a change is feasible can be established by reasoning similar to that employed in the preceding paragraph. The re-allocation of resources will leave u^B unchanged if and only if B's marginal rate of substitution in consumption is equal to the marginal rate of transformation along B's production frontier. This equality must therefore be satisfied in the optimum. From eqs. (8.3) and (8.6), however, we learn that this equality will be established competitively if and only if in B the two commodities are taxed with equal severity:

$$s_1^B = s_2^B. \tag{8.12}$$

As a third example, let $j = B$ in eq. (8.10) and consider a small change in A's production, consumption and trade (with C), with B's production, consumption and trade (with A) held constant. To establish the feasibility of such a re-allocation, consider our system of thirteen equations, with the six policy parameters treated as variables and, this time, with x_i^A and y_i^A fixed at their new sub-optimal levels. As in our first two examples, we have two degrees of freedom. One of these may be used to hold constant relative retail price in B:

$$s_2^B\{(1 + \tau_2^{AB})(1 + \tau_2^{AB*})\}\{(1 + \tau_1^{BA})(1 + \tau_1^{BA*})\}p_2^A/s_1^B p_1^A = \text{const.}$$

In view of eq. (8.12), which uses the remaining degree of freedom, relative prices to B's producers also are constant:

$$\{(1 + \tau_2^{AB})(1 + \tau_2^{AB*})\}\{(1 + \tau_1^{BA})(1 + \tau_1^{BA*})\}p_2^A/p_1^A = \text{const.}$$

It follows that eqs. (8.3) and (8.6) continue to be satisfied by the old x_i^B and y_i^B, that is, that B's production, consumption and trade are unchanged. We may be sure therefore that the hypothetical re-allocation is feasible. Now u^A will be undisturbed by the change if and only if A's marginal rate of substitution in consumption is equal to the rate at which, by moving along A's production frontier and along C's offer curve, one commodity may be converted into the other; that is, if and only if eq. (A5) of the appendix, with $(1 + \tau_2^{AC*})(1 + \tau_1^{CA})$ substituted for β is satisfied. We know, however, that when this product is fixed at less than its Edgeworth-Bickerdike value,

$$s_2^A/s_1^A < 1. \tag{A6}$$

Pulling together the conclusions summarized by eqs. (A6), (8.11) and (8.12), it is possible to describe the optimal internal commercial and fiscal policy of the preferential trading community:

$$s_2^A/s_1^A = \{(1 + \tau_2^{AB})(1 + \tau_2^{AB*})\}\{(1 + \tau_1^{BA})(1 + \tau_1^{BA*})\} < 1 = s_2^B/s_1^B. \tag{8.13}$$

It will be noticed that (8.13) places restrictions only on the *ratio* of consumption taxes in each member country and on the *product* of the internal tariff rates. Mathematically, this merely reflects the fact that in the basic equations, eqs. (8.2)–(8.7), those taxes and duties appear only in ratio or product form. As economists, we may reflect that all effects of a consumption tax on one commodity can be reproduced by a suitable subsidy to the other commodity, and that all effects of a duty imposed by A on B's exports can be reproduced by a suitable tariff on A's exports to B (combined, of course, with a suitable background adjustment to the system of intermember lump-sum transfers). Without implying any loss of effectiveness of its policy instruments, therefore, we could have assumed from the outset that the community has power to tax the consumption of just one commodity, say the first, and power to impose an import *or* export duty on intermember trade in one direction only, say on A's imports from B. If that had been done, the interpretation of (8.13) would have been very simple. The failure of the external tariff to optimally restrict the external trade of the community should be offset by tax discrimination in A against the first or imported commodity. The gap thus opened between the marginal rates of substitution in A and B should be reduced by the subsidization by A of its imports from B. The net effect would be to leave intact the Paretian equalities between the two marginal rates of substitution and B's marginal rate of transformation. Thus the inability to equate the marginal rate of transformation through foreign trade to the several internal marginal rates of substitution and transformation forces the community to breach only one additional Paretian equality – that between the marginal rates of substitution and transformation in the member country which in the conventionally constrained optimum trades with the rest of the world.[8])

8.2.2. A community of similar[9]) countries

If in the optimum both member countries import the first commodity from C, with no net trade between members, matters are very much simpler. Lump-sum transfers between members ensure that the community behaves like a single individual, so that the results of the appendix concerning the optimal vector of consumption taxes may be applied without modification. It is optimal for the community to impose consumption taxes which discriminate against the first or imported commodity, the taxes to be imposed at the same rate in each member country:[10])

$$s_2^A/s_1^A = s_2^B/s_1^B < 1. \tag{8.14}$$

Whether the community imposes tariffs on internal trade is of no significance because, by assumption, the members do not trade with each other.

8.2.3. Policy-making with tariff-discrimination outlawed

In deriving the policy formulae (8.13) and (8.14) it was assumed that the community is free to practise tariff discrimination. Suppose that discrimination is outlawed. Evidently this additional convention is quite ineffective if in the optimum both members import the same commodity, that is, if the members are similar countries. In the alternative case, the same conclusion may be established; but it is rather less obvious.

We revert to the assumption that in the optimum both A and the community as a whole import the first commodity, with B trading only with A. With discrimination outlawed, τ_1^{BA} must be kept equal to τ_1^{CA} and τ_2^{AB*} to τ_2^{AC*}. Since τ_1^{CA} and τ_2^{AC*} are already bound by convention, the community is restricted to six (instead of eight) policy instruments: τ_2^{AB}, τ_1^{BA*} and the s_i^j. However, we know that it is only the products $\{(1 + \tau_2^{AB})(1 + \tau_2^{AB*})\}$ and $\{(1 + \tau_1^{BA})(1 + \tau_1^{BA*})\}$ that matter and these, by assumption,[11]) are not effectively bound. We may conclude, therefore, that the community will be quite unhampered by the constraints imposed on τ_1^{BA} and τ_2^{AB*}. For the outlawing of discrimination to hamper the community it must be coupled with additional restrictions on the internal fiscal policies available to the community. For example, the community might be constrained to levy consumption taxes at the same rate in both member countries. This possibility will be examined in section 8.3.

8.3. Optimal policy with bounds on tariffs: the special cases of free trade associations and customs unions

Throughout our discussion in section 8.2 it was assumed that tariffs on trade between members are included in the armoury of fiscal and commercial devices available to the preferential trading community. It was shown there that a preferential trading community equipped with consumption taxes does not need to engage in tariff discrimination. Hence, even if such a community were subject to a convention like the GATT it would have no incentive to turn itself into a free trade association or customs union. In the present section, therefore, we simply assume that the preferential trading community is subject to the additional constraint that all inter-member trade is free, and then seek the optimal set of consumption taxes.

It sometimes is required, by definition of free trade association or customs union, that the same set of commodity taxes prevail in each member country. In the present case, however, such a requirement would not be binding; for it will be shown that in the absence of internal tariffs it is optimal to impose the same set of consumption taxes in all member countries. Given this finding, it will not be found surprising that the optimal sales tax discriminates against whichever commodity is imported by the preferential trading community.

8.3.1. A community of dissimilar countries

Suppose that in the optimum both A and the preferential trading community as a whole import the first commodity, with B trading only with A. As in section 8.1 we must assume that, as far as trade with C is concerned, the conventional bounds on tariffs are effective. Consider our system of eqs. (8.1)–(8.10), with

$$\tau_1^{BA} = \tau_1^{BA*} = \tau_2^{AB} = \tau_2^{AB*} = 1. \tag{8.15}$$

Let $j = B$ in eq. (8.10) and imagine a small movement along the relevant B-indifference curve with equal but opposite changes in A's consumption, all other variables of the system unchanged. To establish the feasibility of such a change, we note first that with the x_i^j ($j = A, B; i = 1, 2$) fixed at their new values and the four consumption taxes treated as variables, we still have thirteen equations in thirteen variables. Moreover, the initial equilibrium values p_2^A/p_1^A, y_i^j and x_i^C satisfy eqs. (8.1) and (8.4)–(8.9); eq. (8.10) is satisfied by the fixed x_i^B; and eqs. (8.2) and (8.3) are satisfied if the s_1^j/s_2^j are unchanged. Thus the proposed re-allocation is indeed feasible. If now the initial equilibrium is optimal for the community, u^A must be left unchanged by the manoeuvre. This requires that the marginal rates of substitution in A and B be equal. Under competitive conditions this is possible only if each commodity is taxed at the same rate in both member countries:

$$s_1^A/s_2^A = s_1^B/s_2^B. \tag{8.16}$$

It remains only to show that in the optimum $s_1^j < s_2^j$ ($j = A, B$). Given eqs. (8.15) and (8.16), however, that inequality follows from formula (A6) of the appendix.[12])

8.3.2. A community of similar countries

Suppose, finally, that in the optimum both member countries import the first commodity from C. Lump-sum transfers within the community ensure that, if consumption taxes are levied at the same rate in each member country, the community behaves like a single individual. From inequality (A6) of the appendix therefore we may infer that the optimal policy consists in imposing consumption taxes, at the same rate in each member country, which discriminate against the imported commodity. The common external tariffs will of course stand at their upper bounds.

Thus optimal policy takes the same form whether members of the community are similar or dissimilar. This stands in sharp contrast to our findings in section 8.2. The explanation is as follows. In the absence of internal tariffs there is no reason for the community to impose consumption taxes which discriminate between members. Hence the community always behaves like a single individual. Whether or not the members are similar, therefore, the community is bound by the policy inequality (A6).

NOTES

[1]) The wording has been carefully chosen; for the real effects of any tariff, even of an Edgeworth-Bickerdike optimal tariff, can be reproduced by a carefully chosen pair of consumption and production taxes. For details, see the appendix.

[2]) If the production set is rectangular, both consumption tax and import duty touch consumption only; the two taxes are therefore identical in their economic effects. It follows that a conventional restriction on the rate of import duty can be completely offset by taxing at an appropriate rate the consumption of the imported commodity. To deny the community the use of production taxes will in this case not hamper it in the slightest.

[3]) It should be noted that dissimilarity here relates to the situation reached *after* the adoption of an optimal fiscal-commercial policy.

[4]) This proposition is extremely plausible. A formal proof is therefore omitted.

[5]) From this one should not infer that the apportionment of (say) the product $(1 + \tau_2^{AB})(1 + \tau_2^{AB*})$ between the two component terms is unimportant or irrelevant; for some apportionments may be inconsistent with the conventional bounds on tariffs.

[6]) It follows from eq. (8.11) that if for any reason the community is denied the use of consumption taxes free internal trade is optimal.

[7]) This, and similar statements made in this section and the next, require that the relevant 13×15 matrix of partial derivatives be of full rank when evaluated at the optimal point.

[8]) Here we may confirm a conclusion reached in section 8.1, that if the external tariff is set at its Edgeworth-Bickerdike level the optimal internal policy is to

remove all taxes and duties. Thus suppose that $\beta e^C = 1$, where $\beta \equiv (1 + \tau_1{}^{CA})$ $(1 + \tau_2{}^{AC*})$. Then, from eqs. (8.11), (8.12) and (A5),

$$s_2^A/s_1^A = s_2^B/s_1^B = \{(1 + \tau_2^{AB})(1 + \tau_2^{AB*})\}\{(1 + \tau_1^{BA})(1 + \tau_1^{BA*})\} = 1.$$

It follows that within the preferential trading community all relative prices, and therefore all relative rates of substitution and transformation, are the same. Trade between members is essentially free, one country's import duty being precisely offset by the others' import subsidy. In the same way, whatever consumption taxes are imposed exactly neutralize each other in their effects on relative prices. For completeness, we may mention also that, if βe^C is fixed at a level greater than unity, eqs. (8.11), (8.12) and (A5) imply that

$$s_2^A/s_1^A = \{(1 + \tau_2^{AB})(1 + \tau_2^{AB*})\}\{(1 + \tau_1^{BA})(1 + \tau_1^{BA*})\} < 1 = s_2^B/s_1^B$$

so that, as one might have expected, the excessively harsh tariff treatment of the first commodity is mitigated by internal tax discrimination by A against the second or exported commodity.

[9]) See note 3.

[10]) For the relevant formula, see note 3 of the appendix.

[11]) Of course the outlawing of discrimination renders this assumption less plausible.

[12]) The appropriate formula may be found in note 3 of the appendix.

APPENDIX

Optimal tariffs and optimal consumption taxes

A.1. Optimal tariffs

The concept of an optimal tariff vector is a familiar one. However, it will be convenient to have before us a statement of the more important formulae, as well as a sketch of their derivations. For this purpose we may confine ourselves to the policy problem faced by a single country, say country A. Suppose that in the optimum A

A's exports of commodity 2
C's imports of commodity 2

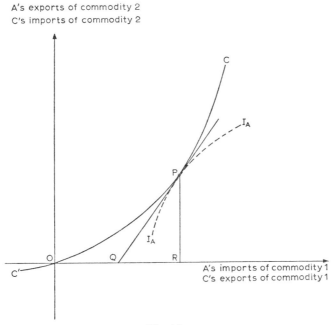

Fig. A1.

imports the first commodity. In fig. A1 COC' is the offer curve of the rest of the world, that is, of C, $I_A I_A$ is one of a family of trade indifference curves for A. The system of external tariffs imposed by A is optimal if it guides trade to the point P where the marginal rate of transformation through trade (indicated by the slope of COC') is equal to the marginal rate of transformation through home production and to the marginal rate of substitution in home consumption. The internal price of the exported commodity (the second) in terms of the imported commodity (the first) is p^A, indicated by the ratio QR/PR. The world price ratio p is, on the other hand, indicated by OR/PR. But $p = p^A(1 + \tau_1^A)(1 + \tau_2^{A*})$, where τ_1^A is the *ad valorem* rate of import duty imposed by A, and τ_2^{A*} is the *ad valorem* rate of export duty. Hence the Edgeworth-Bickerdike optimal mixture of import and export duties is defined by the equation

$$\tau_1^A + \tau_2^{A*} + \tau_1^A \tau_2^{A*} = (p/p^A) - 1$$
$$= \text{OQ/OR} \tag{A1a}$$

which, necessarily, is positive.

Let x_i^C stand for foreign consumption of the ith commodity and y_i^C for foreign production of the ith commodity. Then $(x_i^C - y_i^C)$ stands for the foreign import demand for the ith good and we may define the elasticity of the foreign offer curve as

$$e^C = \frac{y_2^C - x_2^C}{y_1^C - x_1^C} \cdot \frac{d(y_1^C - x_1^C)}{d(y_2^C - x_2^C)}. \tag{A2}$$

It is not difficult to show that OQ/OR is equal to $(1 - e^C)/e^{C.1})$ Thus eq. (A1a) can be written as

$$\tau_1^A + \tau_2^{A*} + \tau_1^A \tau_2^{A*} = (1 - e^C)/e^C > 0. \tag{A1b}$$

Fig. A2 is the graphical counterpart to eq. (A1b). (The left-hand branch of the curve is, of course, quite uninteresting since it fails to satisfy the higher order conditions for a maximum.)

This is the central formula of the theory of optimal tariffs. It will be noticed that the vector of optimal tariffs is not unique: it is possible to assign either rate of duty an arbitrary value, positive or negative, and then read off the optimal value of the other rate from eq. (A1b).[2]) In particular, if one rate of duty is equated to zero the other is equal to

$$(1 - e^{c})/e^{c} \qquad\qquad i = 1 \text{ or } 2. \qquad\qquad \text{(A1c)}$$

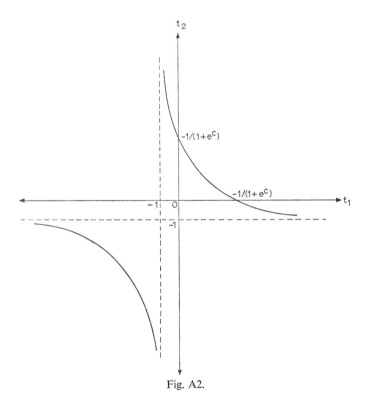

Fig. A2.

There is, however, a more subtle sense in which the optimal tariff vector lacks uniqueness. The value of e^{c} depends on the point on the foreign offer curve at which an evaluation is made. The relevant point depends on A's indifference map, and the latter reflects the distribution of income within A. There is therefore not a single graph of optimal tariff pairs but an infinity; even when an arbitrary value is assigned to one tariff the optimal value of the other emerges only when the distribution of income within A is known. Finally, we recall that in deriving eq. (A1) we implicitly assumed that within A all commodity taxes are equated to zero. In fact, however, that is only one of many ways in which competitive trade and communal welfare can be driven to the optimum. As fig. A1 illustrates, an essential characteristic of the optimum is an (optimal) gap between the internal and external price ratios, with the same internal price ratio for consumers and producers. It is clear, however, that the same gap can be created, without resort to tariffs, by imposing in A a consumption tax and a production subsidy on the imported commodity, both the tax and the subsidy at the Edgeworth-Bickerdike rate $(1 - e^{C})/e^{C}$; or by imposing a consumption subsidy and a production tax on the exported commodity, again at the same rate $(1 - e^{C})/e^{C}$. And evidently the same ultimate effects could be achieved by all kinds of hybrid commercial-fiscal policies. Thus we have yet another reason for denying the uniqueness of the optimal tariff vector.

A.2. Optimal consumption taxes

We conclude this appendix by considering a problem closely related to that of finding the optimal tariff vector. Suppose that the external tariff vector of A is rigidly fixed, by international convention, at a less-than-optimal level, so that it can be represented by a point below the right-hand curve of fig. A2; suppose further that A's battery of fiscal devices is limited to taxes on consumption. The problem is to find the optimal vector of consumption taxes. Since the duties imposed on foreign trade are insufficiently restrictive one would expect that it would be optimal to discriminate against the consumption of the first or imported commodity. This expectation will be confirmed.

In A the price of the ith commodity as seen by producers differs by the amount of the consumption tax from the price as seen by consumers. Clearly p_i^A cannot stand for both prices. In what follows p_i^A will stand for the producers' price in A; s_i^A will stand for one plus the *ad valorem* rate of consumption tax in A; and, therefore, $s_i^A p_i^A$ will stand for the consumers' price in A. The product of one plus the rate of import duty imposed by A and one plus the rate of export duty imposed by A will be denoted by β:

$$(1 + \tau_1^A)(1 + \tau_2^{A*}) = \beta$$

β is, of course, a constant. Suppose that s_1^A and s_2^A have been set at their optimal levels and that an international equilibrium has been established. Then any infinitesimal and feasible change in the quantities produced, consumed and traded by the two countries must leave A's utility unchanged. Now the utility of A will be undisturbed by the change if and only if A's marginal rate of substitution in consumption is equal to the rate at which, by moving along A's production frontier and along C's offer curve, one commodity may be converted into the other. The second of these two rates is equal to

$$\frac{dy_1^A + d(y_1^C - x_1^C)}{dy_2^A + d(y_2^C - x_2^C)} \tag{A3a}$$

where y_i^A is the amount of the ith commodity produced by A and $(y_i^C - x_i^C)$ is the amount of the ith commodity exported by C. In view of eq. (A2), expression (A3a) can be written alternatively as

$$\frac{dy_1^A + e^C[(y_1^C - x_1^C)/(y_2^C - x_2^C)] \cdot d(y_2^C - x_2^C)}{dy_2^A + d(y_2^C - x_2^C)}. \tag{A3b}$$

However, balance of payments equilibrium requires that

$$p_1^A(x_1^C - y_1^C) + \beta p_2^A(x_2^C - y_2^C) = 0$$

and A's production equilibrium requires that

$$- \mathrm{d}y_1^A / \mathrm{d}y_2^A = p_2^A / p_1^A.$$

Hence (A3b) can be expressed as

$$- \frac{p_2^A}{p_1^A} \cdot \frac{\mathrm{d}y_2^A + e^C \beta d(y_2^C - x_2^C)}{\mathrm{d}y_2^A + \mathrm{d}(y_2^C - x_2^C)}. \tag{A3c}$$

On the other hand, A's marginal rate of substitution in consumption is equal to minus the ratio of consumers' prices

$$- \frac{p_2^A}{p_1^A} \cdot \frac{s_2^A}{s_1^A}. \tag{A4}$$

Thus, equating expressions (A3c) and (A4), we find that in an optimum[3])

$$\frac{s_2^A}{s_1^A} = \frac{\mathrm{d}y_2^A + \beta e^C d(y_2^C - x_2^C)}{\mathrm{d}y_2^A + \mathrm{d}(y_2^C - x_2^C)}. \tag{A5}$$

Since β is constant, p_1^A / p_2^A and the terms of trade between A and C bear a constant relation to each other; hence $\mathrm{d}y_2^A$ and $\mathrm{d}(y_2^C - x_2^C)$ have the same sign. Moreover, by assumption the external tariffs are fixed at less than their optimal values; that is, $\beta e^C < 1$. Applying these observations to eq. (A5) we conclude that

$$s_2^A / s_1^A < 1. \tag{A6}$$

Thus it is optimal for A to impose consumption taxes which discriminate against the first or imported commodity. The appropriate discrimination can be achieved by taxing consumption of the imported commodity, or by subsidizing consumption of the exported commodity, or by more complicated tax-subsidy pairs; only the ratio of s_2^A to s_1^A matters.

NOTES

[1]) See, for example, Kemp [5], ch. 14.

[2]) Notice that, if the uninteresting left-hand branch of the graph is ignored, at least one element of the optimal tariff vector must be positive. In more general models than those displayed here this is not necessarily true. See Kemp [5], ch. 14.

[3]) Converting to elasticities, and making use of the identity

$$[d(y_2^C - x_2^C)/d(p_2\beta/p_1)][(p_2\beta/p_1)/(y_2^C - x_2^C)] = 1/(e^C - 1),$$

we obtain

$$\frac{s_2^A}{s_1^A} = \frac{1 + \{[e^C/(1 - e^C)] \cdot [\beta/e] \cdot [(y_2^C - x_2^C)/y_{21}^A]\}}{1 + \{[1/(1 - e^C)] \cdot [1/e] \cdot [(y_2^C - x_2^C)/y_{21}^A]\}}$$

where $e = (dy_2^A/dp^A)(p^A/y_2^A)$ is the 'general equilibrium' elasticity of supply of the second commodity in A. This formula for the optimal vector of consumption taxes is the counterpart of the formula (A1b) for the optimal tariff vector.

References

[1] Bhagwati, Jagdish, 'The gains from trade once again', *Oxford Economic Papers*, XX, no. 2 (July 1968), 137–148.

[2] Corden, W. M., 'The structure of a tariff system and the effective protective rate', *Journal of Political Economy*, LXXIV, no. 3 (June 1966), 221–237.

[3] Inada, Ken-ichi and Murray C. Kemp, 'International capital movements and the theory of international trade', *Quarterly Journal of Economics*, LXXXIII, no. 3 (August 1969).

[4] Kemp, Murray C., 'Some issues in the analysis of trade gains', *Oxford Economic Papers*, XX, no. 2 (July 1968), 149–161.

[5] Kemp, Murray C., *The pure theory of international trade and investment*, Englewood Cliffs, N.J.: Prentice-Hall Inc., 1969.

[6] Lipsey, R. G. and Kelvin Lancaster, 'The general theory of second best', *Review of Economic Studies*, XX(1), no. 63 (1956–57), 11–32.

[7] Meade, J. E., *The theory of custom unions*. Amsterdam: North-Holland Publishing Company, 1955.

[8] Negishi, Takashi, 'Customs union and the theory of the second best', *International Economic Review*, to be published.

[9] Vanek, Jaroslav, *General equilibrium of international discrimination*. Cambridge, Mass.: Harvard University Press, 1965.

[10] Viner, Jacob, *The customs union issue*. New York: Carnegie Endowment for International Peace, 1950.

Subject index